Reader Feedback on
Succeed Without Burnout

"I just finished reading Ben Kubassek's book (twice) *Succeed Without Burnout* and a bright light went on in my heart and in my brain. My husband and I have read many "self-help books" trying to find peace and prosperity and to self-improve: Norman Vincent Peale, Tony Robbins, Stephen Covey, Jack Canfield, etc...but I found that Mr. Kubassek's book brought all these principles together in an under-standable, d~~~~ ~~~~ For me it has reawakened my hunger for spiritua'   ."

                                                          , Ontario

"I'm ;   ary with
severe   lequate,
runnin}   ing like
no one   me....I
bought   it away.
I loved   nal, and
easy to   you said
that re;   nesty in
writing

                                                          Ontario

"I ha   to your
audio   of your
semina   ; well as

many others. I have been able to bring my own life into balance by simply practicing the principles you so passionately teach....Your presentation style exemplifies a genuinely caring individual who is committed to helping others achieve the best of life, by teaching them your life balance formula.

Having personally read, studied and experienced many of the leading motivators in today's world, I can confirm that you have a unique way of sharing your message that I'm sure will appeal to the masses. You not only inspire others into action, but also provide them with the day-to-day skills necessary for growth and success..."

Jose F. G. Machado, CEO, Cambridge, Ontario

"*Succeed Without Burnout* is a wonderful book about a purposeful subject. Read it to learn, grow, and nurture your life."

Nido R. Qubein, Chairman, Creative Services

"Your book [*Succeed Without Burnout*] was a quick read—but had a powerful life-changing impact on my entire lifestyle! I was going down a dead-end road to burnout, and reading your book has brought refreshing and much-needed balance to my life. Thank you for your transparency and insights to help so many of us in executive leadership."

George Glover, Executive Director, Teen Challenge Canada

"I recommend *Succeed Without Burnout* to all my clients as good preventative reading toward their overall well-being."

Wilma Bolton, Registered Massage Therapist

"I'd just like to say how much my husband and I have enjoyed your book. It was like a light has come on and we now realize what our problem is. We are just plainly BURNT OUT!"

Wendy Preston, Madoc, Ontario

I received your book [*Succeed Without Burnout*] this week and I cannot thank you enough for your personal efforts. I am nearly through my first read and have found your descriptions hauntingly familiar and your suggestions terrific. The most important thing for me was to realize that I was not the only one....You have shown me this can be beaten; it was critical for me to be convinced there is hope....Thanks again for your book.

David Brimacombe, Australia

It's a book I couldn't put down. I just had to finish it. Reading your words helped me a GREAT deal as I'm sure they have helped countless others. It might not have been easy to write this book, but I'm sure glad you did.

Gloria Krismanick, Ayr, Ontario

I have recently finished reading your book, *Succeed Without Burnout*. I wept openly as I was touched by compassion....You see, my brother, I was cold and bitter for a long time. Guys like me didn't cry. Now, praise God, I cry!

I found myself cheering as you made your comeback to a peace with life. A seed of Burnout entered your life and as a result you harvested a book that will go on to help others heal from, and avoid, Burnout. I wasn't a hugger kind of person; now that wall is all but down completely. Gratitude was never a big thing with me. That too was encouraged much by your book.

Gary Garrity, Teen Challenge Farm

"Thanks for your wise words and thoughts on burnout. Everyone needs to read good material. Input to the brain is very important....Thank you again for your book. I have about a dozen copies in the office for my patients."

Ian A. Judge, D.C., FCCRS(C), London, Ontario

"Over-committed? Burning the candle at both ends? Over-loaded emotionally? Then you need to read *Succeed Without Burnout*. It offers proven strategies to move you from victim to victor!"

Paul J. Meyer, founder—Success Motivation Inc.

Succeed Without Burnout is a must-read book for any harried executive, working mom who feels she's at the threshold, and everyone suffering from the malaise called "Hurry Sickness."

Mark Victor Hansen, co-author, Chicken Soup for the Soul

Succeed Without Burnout is a wonderful, helpful book of practical, proven ways to increase energy, enthusiasm and self-confidence. It can change your entire attitude toward life—for the better!"

Brian Tracey, author, Business Success

Five "F" Words That Will Energize Your Life

Simple steps to move your life from Burnout to Balance

Ben Kubassek

Books that Inspire, Help and Heal

Published by Creative Bound Inc.
Box 424, Carp, Ontario
Canada K0A 1L0
(613) 831-3641

ISBN 0-921165-61-7
Printed and bound in Canada

Book design: Wendelina O'Keefe

Photograph: John Mitchell

Editor: Janet Shorten

printing number 10 9 8 7 6 5 4 3 2 1

Canadian Cataloguing in Publication Data

Kubassek, Ben, 1958-
        Five "F" words that will energize your life

Includes bibliographical references.
ISBN 0-921165-61-7

        1. Self-actualization (Psychology) I. Title.

BF637.S4K82 1999   158.1   C99-900389-5

I dedicate this book to my friends worldwide.
Thanks for enriching my life and reminding me
about what really matters.
Thanks for helping me find the meaning of Real Balance.
I am truly blessed to be able to call you friends.

ACKnoWleDGMents

It takes the combined effort of many to complete a book. It requires an understanding and supportive family. I thank God for mine. Thanks to my wife, Elizabeth, for your endless support. Your faithfulness and love, and our children, have made me a wealthy man. Thanks to my children Krystal, Daniel, Joshua and Jonathan for giving me time alone, when you would have rather spent time together with Dad. Thanks to my Mom and Dad for believing in me. By teaching me to believe in myself and in the God that created me, you gave me the basic tools for success. Thanks again.

Thanks to Gail, Barb and Wendy at Creative Bound for believing in the message I bring to a hurting and stressed-out world. It has been a delight to work as a team with a common purpose: "To inspire, help and heal." What an awesome mission. Together we will make the world a better place.

Thanks to all the people who bought my first book. You made me a best-selling author. Thank you.

contents

InTRODUCTiON

See if these examples don't sound familiar:

Derrick is a high-profile branch manager with a big city financial institution. Helen is a nurse, a single working person many of her friends label Super Mom. Tom is a minister in a small rural community with 300 devoted parishioners. And Melanie is a university student, aiming to become an architect.

These people all live hundreds of miles apart, in situations as different as you could possibly imagine. But they all have one thing in common. All of them, whether they recognize it or not, are on the verge of becoming victims of BURNOUT.

Derrick is a high-energy, highly motivated financier. He is driven to do well for himself and his company. But he's a perfectionist, working overly long hours, unwilling or unable to delegate. He's at his desk 18 hours a day, often eating his lunch while dictating memos. Everything he does is at warp speed, including the few minutes each week he spends with his family.

Helen, on the other hand, deals with emotions, sickness and hardship every day at her hospital post. Then she races to daycare to pick up the kids, throws dinner together, does the dishes, cleans the kitchen, makes lunches and helps the youngsters with their homework, before finally dropping into bed exhausted.

All his parishioners love Tom; they call him day and night with their problems. He organizes most of the social events in his community, and seems always eager and ready to volunteer. But his wife and kids rarely see him, his resentful teenage son is drinking underage, and his twin daughters are both struggling with their grades. His community contributions have come at the expense of home life, and he is starting to recognize that. But how can he turn his back on so many people?

Melanie knew that architecture would be difficult. She was always a good student, but nobody had prepared her for the need to study seven days a week, virtually around the clock. Sleep isn't possible, not with that deadline looming at 9 a.m. Monday. Friends? She barely sees them. She has become a prisoner at her own study desk.

Like Tom, Helen and Derrick, Melanie is being swallowed up by a mysterious affliction. It's called BURNOUT. And it can affect anyone, even those least expecting it. Trust me. That's my life story. I'm both a burnout victim, and one who, after desperate times, recognized what was missing in my life, what I needed to do to recover, and how to move my life from burnout to balance. Remember those words, because you'll read them often through the course of this book. Burnout. Balance. Burnout. Balance.

When I published *Succeed Without Burnout*, it was my own account detailing my personal struggle with burnout, but more importantly, chronicling my recovery from it. In that book, I talk about how I turned my life around from the brink of self-destruction to once again become a devoted family man, community leader and a person making a difference to thousands of people around the world. This book, with real-life stories, is the perfect complement to *Succeed Without Burnout*. I'm confident that, as we take a deeper look at the ingredients of a happy, fulfilled and balanced life, you too will discover Real Balance. I believe this book will make a difference in your life. I'm honored to be your guide, to lead the way along the path from burnout to balance. My mission is to serve you, to provide you with a road map to inner peace, a sense of purpose, direction, balance and true happiness.

Am I a success? In many ways, absolutely. But there is no pedestal I stand on. Quite the opposite, my feet are firmly planted on the ground. You see, recovering from burnout, keeping our life in balance, is something you and I have to work hard at, every living day, every breathing moment. If we don't, the elevator door, or the roller coaster ride, is waiting right around the corner to take us from the highest high to the lowest low. By recognizing the signs of burnout, and taking the steps necessary to avoid it, we create a smoother ride, and a powerful sense that we are in balance, in control. Life will always have its ups and downs; it's how we deal with them that charts our course, that personal road map I talk about.

Since publishing *Succeed Without Burnout*, I've heard two comments again and again. One is that readers identify with the book, whether they see themselves, a close family member, a friend or a business associate. Secondly, they express their admiration to me for baring my soul, not skimming over the raw, gut-wrenching times I experienced. And for telling my story on those pages, illustrating that there is HOPE for all of us. I knew that without hope, I had no possibility of recovery. I had big goals for my life. I needed reassurance that after having met virtually all of them at such an early age there was something more to live for. Especially in the lowest times, when I felt wretched, couldn't sleep, heck—I couldn't function. In the process of recovery, I discovered there was hope, there was so much to live for, so much more for me to accomplish in life. Readers of my first book have told me they respect what I have to say, because I am not preaching from on high, but because I have been there, done that.

As with other self-help and teaching tools, my experience has taught me that in achieving Real Balance there is a formula to follow. I call my formula the Five "F" Words. Now, you may think that an F is a terrible grade, a sign of failure. Some people even think every "F" word is dirty. I'm here to tell you that those five "F" words—Fitness, Family, Friends, Finances and Faith—when treated in balance, are instead a recipe for a fulfilling, rewarding life. A life of Total Prosperity.

It is far simpler to analyze, now, the reason for my burnout, than it was in those horrid first moments when I suffered from it. Simply stated, I had achieved significant early success in business, and I craved the adrenaline rush that reaching self-imposed goals created.

So I kept moving the bar higher, and the adrenaline rushes fueled the next round. But in trying to reach those goals, I was ignoring the elements that compose the five "F" words. I had little or no time for family or friends, shunned physical and recreational activities, and abandoned my faith. As I became a success in business, I became a failure in all other aspects of my life.

What I also didn't know was that burnout was lurking in the shadows. And like the proverbial horror movie, when it jumped out to seize me, it was my worst nightmare come true.

In the following pages, I will guide you through the methods I use in achieving Real Balance, and more importantly, maintaining that precious balance. For me, that balance restored my zest for life, gave me hope for the future, and gave me a renewed feeling that I was in control. If these methods do the same for you, then my purpose will have been served. As I told a friend recently, "I've spent much of my life building homes. I want to spend the rest of my life building people." But before we look at the five "F" words, each the topic of its own chapter, I'd like to share some my life experiences with you, and the story of moving my own life from Burnout to Balance, the one so many of my readers say they identify with. Although I'm not sure how many of them made their first big career decision while spreading chicken manure…

PART ONE: THERE MUST BE A BETTER WAY!

Everyone wants it. Few achieve it. Balance: It's the Holy Grail in the new world of work....How do you pursue your work goals and still stay connected to the things that make you human?[1]

Fast Company Magazine

Following a Dream

"Those who are at war with others are not at peace
with themselves."

William Hazlitt (1778-1830)

As he sat huddled in that cold, dark trench with bombs exploding
all around him the young Hungarian soldier thought to himself, "there
must be a better way to live." That young Hungarian soldier fighting
in the First World War was my grandfather, the late Julius John
Kubassek. As he crawled out of the trench he had spent the night in,
he quickly realized that only two other soldiers had survived the
attack. They had both spent the night in the same trench he had; one
had been on his left, the other on his right. That was all he could take.
He was fed up with the war and all the killing that was going on. He
kept thinking to himself, "there must be a better way." Fed up, he stuck
the bayonet of his gun into the ground and refused to take up arms
from that moment on. He defected from the Hungarian army. He chose
to follow his convictions rather than follow the orders he was given.

As my grandfather spent the next six weeks hiding in a cave under
the pigpen on his parents' farm, he started to do some serious thinking. He began to think about the war and how a God who had created all of us certainly would not condone our killing each other. He
also began to read the New Testament. As he studied the Book of Acts
he realized that the members of the first church had lived together
and had all things in common. No one called anything their own.

Wow, he thought, "what a concept." if we lived that way today there would be no need for war. That was certainly a better way in his mind. That was it. That immediately became his dream, to find such a place, a place of peace and harmony where everyone lived together and shared all things.

A dream without a plan is as useless as a plan without action.

He realized a dream without a plan was useless. He realized that a plan without action was just as useless. However, taking action means choice. Taking no action is also a choice; it's choosing to do nothing. He could choose to stay with his family and his familiar surroundings, or he could choose to follow his dream. Even though it meant taking a great risk, he chose to follow his dream. So one night he left his family and friends and his homeland, in search of his dream, running at night and hiding in the woods by day.

When my grandfather finally reached the border he was stopped by a guard and asked for his travel papers. Unable to produce the correct documents, he simply asked the guard if he had anything better. Miraculously, the guard gave my grandfather his own papers, allowing him to cross the border into Austria. It's amazing what happens when we know our purpose, have a plan and are persistent in following it. It's also amazing what happens when you ask.

In search of his dream he began to attend a Baptist church in Vienna, where he brought up his idea of living together and sharing earthly possessions. The people in the church thought it was a great idea and suggested he travel to America where there was plenty of wealth, get a job, and bring back to Austria enough money to buy land and start a commune. It never ceases to amaze me how many people will act on a plan as long as someone else takes the risk. They will gladly follow someone else's dream. It's a lot safer that way. At the same time they wonder why their lives lack purpose, passion and a sense of fulfillment. Grandpa wasn't about to let his dream die. If following his dream meant sailing to a country he knew very little about except that it was a land of opportunity, he would do it. It didn't matter if he couldn't speak, had little money and no contacts. He had faith in himself and he had faith in God. He didn't need any more than that.

With purpose, passion and persistence we can overcome any obstacle we face in life.

By the time my grandfather arrived in America it was the 1930s and he couldn't buy a job. He spent weeks walking from one factory to the next, asking if they had a job for him. But he was not about to give up after he had come this far; besides, he had only purchased a one-way ticket to America. There was no going back, so he decided to check out the possibilities in Canada. He walked across Ambassador Bridge on foot, and he applied for and got a job at Ford Motor Company as a tool and die maker. He finally had the job he had come so far to find. Many times in life, we are just one bridge away from success. We give up because we lose sight of our purpose. Grandpa had been persistent; he never gave up in his search for his dream—a place of harmony and peace, a place where people lived together and shared all things. Not finding his dream, he created it. In 1940, with a net worth of 6 cents and a vendor who offered 100 percent financing, my grandfather purchased a 200-acre farm near Kitchener, Ontario, and there he founded the Community Farm of the Brethren. His dream had come true!

THE SIMPLE LIFE

I was the middle one of seven children, and I can tell you we had a very simple lifestyle growing up on the Farm. How simple was it? Let's just say we had a-pail-a-day system sewage facilities and we kids shared the same bathwater in the old steel tub my mom got down every Saturday. We grew our own food and made our own clothes. There was no TV, radio or newspaper allowed on the Farm. Grandpa believed we needed to keep the influence of the outside world to a minimum.

The Farm was made up of 16 families living, working and sharing together. We were one big happy family of 120 men, women and children living on one farm, eating our meals together in the common dining room, worshiping together in the chapel, sharing an automobile and all living out of the same bank account. Most importantly, we all had the same values of sharing, caring and peace. We believed that if we planted the seed God would give the increase. God never gives a harvest; he only gives seed and His blessing. If we didn't do our part of cultivating, fertilizing and watering, we still wouldn't have a harvest. Real prosperity is a joint-venture relationship between the Creator and the created. These timeless biblical principles would prove to be invaluable to me in the future.

> **"How good and how pleasant it is when brethren live together in unity!"**
> Psalm 133:1

Since the community was very closed to the outside world and very self-sustaining, we seldom left the premises, not even for school. We got our education right there on the farm. I completed my formal studies by the age of 14 in the two-room schoolhouse that my father had built. Even though I loved to learn, had the top marks and enjoyed school a great deal, education beyond Grade 8 was considered to be unnecessary and was not encouraged on the farm. I wanted to continue my education when I graduated from Grade 8, but wasn't old enough to take correspondence courses.

You have heard the expression "timing is everything," and it certainly was for me. As our first shoemaker retired and then a month later the chicken man left the farm—take a guess who got both those jobs. Well, everyone looked at young Ben Kubassek and said, "this kid can do anything," and so at that tender age I accepted a great deal of responsibility. They were, in effect, grooming me to inherit my father's position as manager. I was the only guy who didn't have to stand in line each morning after breakfast to get an assignment for the day—the truth is, I probably had more planned for that day than most of them did for the entire week. I would soon learn that the whole world won't stop a person with purpose and a sense of direction and self-confidence.

What you are is God's gift to you. What you will become (not what you will achieve) will be your gift to God.

Although I was being brought up in a communist environment, I believed myself to be born a capitalist. Each and every day I took on my heavy load, but kept saying to myself, "There must be a better way. I was born for more than this!" My mom kept reminding me: "What you are, son, is God's gift to you. What you will someday become will be your gift to God." I was determined I would become all I could be. And if God really was watching, I wanted to put on a good show.

We all have defining moments in our lives. One of mine came one day when I was spreading liquid chicken manure. It was a windy day, and I had always been curious to know what would happen if you turned downwind on a windy day. So I took a look back. Not the wisest move I'd ever made. That very day, as I sat on that farm tractor, drenched in chicken manure, I said to myself, "That's it, it's time to seek the better way." By the age of 16, I was sure of it, believing that somehow I could use the potential I had in me to a much greater degree in a free enterprise system. If I had my own way, I could be the capitalist I had always wanted to be.

Have fun at what you are doing, or do something else.

OUR CHOICES DETERMINE OUR FUTURE

In life we all face many choices every day. It was time to make the biggest decision of my life. I knew I needed to make a choice between staying on the Farm with my family, my friends and the financial security that communal living provided, or stepping out and following my dream. I needed to make a choice between following my grandfather's dream and following my own dream. I knew that my choice would determine my future. I also knew that the easiest decision would be to decide to do nothing. And, somewhere deep inside, I knew I needed to follow my own dream. So I began to plan to leave the Farm.

GETTING FIRED UP

At this point in time I began to prepare to leave the Farm by taking a used home-study course for electricians. I also read every self-help book I could get my hands on. The more I prepared, the more passionate I became. That passion began to fuel the fire within me. The more I learned about the electrical trade the more convinced I was I could be a success in the outside world.

Earning a dollar a day on the Farm, the same wage everyone else made, I was licensed by the age of 21. Now everything didn't just happen helter-skelter when I left the farm on January 1, 1980. I had let my family know a couple of months before that I wasn't happy there and that I would be leaving. I knew it wouldn't be easy, but the thought kept entering my mind: "There has to be a better way."

LIGHTS, CAMERA, ACTION

So on January 1, 1980, armed with my plan, my purpose and my passion—oh, and let's not forget my Grade 8 education and $2,000 in my pocket—I left the Community Farm of the Brethren. I left my family, I left my friends, I left my financial security, and as far as the farm people were concerned I left my faith. I was also leaving behind Elizabeth, the girl of my dreams.

I had mixed feelings as I left that frosty January morning. On one hand I was excited about leaving the Farm, and on the other hand it hurt to see how broken-hearted my parents were to see their son leaving the Farm and venturing out into the world. The child they had taught to love, to give and to care had chosen the way of the world. But it was my life, it was my dream and I was going to follow it.

Ben Kubassek was ready to take the world by storm. I believed in myself and I believed in the God that had created me. I thought I could do anything, have anything or be anything, and I wasn't going to let anything get in my way. I didn't. I believed I could do anything I wanted to, if I wanted to bad enough. I could have anything, if I wanted it bad enough. I could become anything, if I wanted to bad enough. I was now a free man, in a free country, a land of opportunity. Nothing and no one could stop me now. My only limit was my imagination.

My lack of education wasn't going to stop me, I'd continue to read and study every self-help book I could get my hands on. When I was in my vehicle I'd listen to teaching tapes instead of the radio. All the information I needed was available to me; I could even get books from the library without having to buy them. I could learn anything if I wanted to bad enough.

My lack of experiences and contacts wouldn't stop me. It hadn't stopped my Grandpa; he simply followed his dream and he couldn't even speak English when he arrived at his land of opportunity. Look at what he accomplished, I told myself. I could get experience if I was determined and wanted it bad enough.

The fact that I was leaving the farm with $2,000 wasn't going to stop me. I went right into business. I was used to earning a dollar a day and I knew that I was worth more than that. I believed that the world would compensate me in direct proportion to the value I brought to it, as long as I didn't limit myself by looking for a job. I would take the same energy and invest it looking for customers. The fact that the country was in recession wouldn't stop me from starting a business with my oldest brother. We didn't have any overhead expenses and we could beat anyone's price.

I began to realize that everything in my situation that appeared to be a liability was actually an asset. Wow, the only difference was how

I perceived the situation and my attitude toward it. So I toiled long and hard, and I laid the foundation for those memorable "magic touch" days of business when it seemed everything I touched turned to gold. And what a feeling it was…

EVERYTHING I TOUCHED

Within a year of my leaving the Farm and going into business with my oldest brother, we found ourselves in the midst of the 1981-82 recession. Dave had left the Farm eight years earlier at the ripe age of 16. He had served an apprenticeship as a plumber and was tired of working for someone else. Times were tight and it was difficult to find enough work to keep us busy. But I wasn't going to let a little thing like a recession stand between my dreams and me. One of my dreams was to build my own home. Not just any home—I wanted a raised brick ranch-style bungalow with white pillars across the front. This home would be located on an acreage that I could develop into a hobby farm with a barn for my horses and a hangar for the helicopter I would one day own.

When I had left home at the age of 21, I was determined to become a financial success. I would do whatever it took to reach my goals, all of which at the time were financial. One of the goals I set was to become a millionaire by the age of 50. I would then retire and enjoy life. Within six years I had achieved every goal I had set for my entire life: a beautiful wife, an adorable family and the home of my dreams on a hobby farm. I was driving a luxury automobile, owned three businesses and had a net worth in excess of one million dollars. I had literally gone from the henhouse to Who's Who.

THE POWER OF PURPOSE

If I held up a fork and asked you, "what's the purpose of this?" you would probably say, "it's a utensil we use to feed ourselves." If I held up an axe and asked, "what is the purpose of this object?" you would probably say, "that's a tool we use to cut wood." Why is it then that when you ask people what their purpose is, it's so difficult to get an answer? We know the purpose of everything around us, but we don't know what purpose our lives serve. Why are you here? What purpose does your life serve in making this world a better place? What purpose do you serve in your family? Your community? Your business? Perhaps you have been asking yourself those questions throughout your life and have come up blank. How then do we determine our purpose?

Think about it for a moment. Who determines the purpose of any object? Is it the user, or is it the inventor? Of course it is the inventor that determines purpose; it is the user that determines how the invention will be put to use. Just the same, our inventor (or Creator) determined our purpose when we were created in our mother's womb. How we use our life (or use up our time) here on earth is *our* call. The value we place on ourselves and our time is up to us. It's called *choice*. We can choose many things in life, but we cannot choose our purpose. We cannot *choose* our purpose; we can only *understand* our purpose. Well, that's great, but how do we understand what our purpose is? What was it our Creator had in mind when He created us with our billion-dollar body and our creative mind so powerful we only use 1/100 of 1 percent of its capacity?

Don't worry, I'm not going to get religious on you, but you need to understand that we are spiritual beings having a physical experience if you are ever going to understand your purpose. Ask the religious folks and they'll tell you: "That's easy, just ask God; He made you. Pray and ask Him what purpose He had in mind for you." Those are the same people wandering through life following someone else's tail lights to work every morning without a clue about why they were placed on this planet. I believe in prayer and asking for wisdom on a daily basis, but I believe the answer to the question "what is my purpose?" has already been given and lies within each one of us waiting to be discovered.

If you didn't know the purpose for a tool in your toolbox or a utensil in your kitchen you'd probably throw it out. Not knowing the purpose of an object makes that object of no value to you. It's as if that object was worthless. Many times valuable objects are discarded simply because their purpose is not known to the owner. That's why many lives are thrown away. The people who own them don't know their purpose. Do you know what your purpose is? Do you know why the good Lord placed you here on this earth? If not, I hope by the time you finish this book you have a better idea.

People who lack purpose seldom have a life plan. Why have plans for something that has no purpose? It wouldn't make any sense! There is a fulfillment that comes when you begin to follow a plan that is aligned with your purpose. I had a plan for my life and I was passionately following it. At the time I left the commune, I believed my purpose was to become an incredible success in business. The plan, or the map, I was following was taking me there. However, as we will see in the next chapter there are times we are following the wrong map. The map I was following was leading me to tremendous success in business, but at the same time was leading me toward failure in many other areas of my life. I had only part of the picture of what my purpose truly was. It was much more than becoming a financial success. The bad news was I was heading in the wrong direction; the good news was I was making great time!

Whether the goal or destination is the right one, if we stay focused we will arrive. The power of purpose is the strongest force that can ever be at work within us. It has the ability to destroy and conquer, as we have seen with some leaders in the past. Having visited the country of Romania some eight times since the revolution took place there, I have seen first-hand the power of purpose in the mind of an evil leader, their president Ceaucescu. On the one hand I admire his tremendous achievements and ability to lead people, but on the other hand I've been appalled at the toll his purpose took in human lives. Visiting an orphanage or hospital with hundreds of children dying from Aids and experiencing for just 30 minutes the misery and hopelessness of their situation is enough to remind anyone that we all need to be certain we are following the right plan for our lives.

I'll never forget one little five-year-old boy in particular. His mother had dropped him off the day before I visited the hospital for kids with Aids in Constanta, Romania, abandoning him like so many other parents have done. As my friend Keith Gonyou, who had accompanied me on this particular trip, picked him up from his crib, this little guy threw his arms around Keith's neck, and began babbling in Romanian and refusing to let go.

I turned to our translator to get the English version of what was going down. Our translator responded, "He's saying God has sent us to take him home." How do you tell a five-year-old he can't go home? Not now. Not ever. I watched as tears filled Keith's eyes and he turned to me and said, "Ben, get me out of here. I can't handle this." The pain caused by the choices made by an evil leader was unbearable to watch.

Following the wrong map can lead to disaster. It can ruin our health, destroy our families and lead to disaster. The plan I was following was leading me to a dead-end called BURNOUT.

Tо Hell and Back

"What shall it profit a man, if he gain the whole world, and lose his own soul?"[2] (Or his own health, or his own family for that matter?)

People with purpose have clearly defined long-term goals. People with goals spend time in preparing themselves and their teams to reach those goals. They have faith. Faith in themselves, in others and in God. Not only do they have faith, but also their faith has matured to the point where they take action. They never stop growing. People without a plan seldom spend much time in preparation and most stop growing. They don't persist in time of difficulty. They have no goal on which to keep their eyes. They lack focus and are easily sidetracked.

The shortest path between any goal and us is the straightest line possible. I remember back on the farm getting my first lesson on plowing a straight furrow. Brother Alex, the gardener, would say to me, "If you want to plow a straight furrow, always pick an object in the distance to focus on. Don't look at the ground in front of the tractor but rather the focal point you picked at the end of the field." He warned me, though, never to focus on an object that could move, such as a grazing cow. What a lesson for life. It's easy to keep our path straight if we stay focused on our purpose. Otherwise, we jump from one get-rich scheme to another, from one relationship to another.

Purpose is the fuel that feeds the fire of our passion.

The power of purpose in our lives is the fuel that feeds our passion and drives us toward the achievement of the goals we've set for our lives. However, simply being aware of our purpose is not enough in itself, we need an igniter to light the fire. It is the planning and preparation that ignites the passion in passionate people. With passion every day is a blessing. We are glad to be alive. We find it difficult to separate play and work. Passionate people are always more prosperous. They are higher achievers and bursting with energy. They focus on the positive and what is right with the world. They talk about what they are for and not what they are against. They know that everything we are for, empowers us, and everything we're against, disempowers us.

Passion with balance is the key to Total Prosperity.

Many passionate people, including myself, as I was about to discover, achieve tremendous success in business at the expense of their health, their family and their faith. They mortgage their families to pay the price for their financial success. They mortgage their health to leverage their own physical limitations in an attempt to satisfy their boss. Mortgage means a conveyance or giving of property (as for security on a loan) on condition that the conveyance becomes void (in other words, we get it back) on payment or performance according to stipulated terms of the mortgage. It is one way we can leverage our assets. However, we sometimes are mortgaging assets without even realizing it.

The worst scenario is mortgaging our families or health to increase the size of our paycheck and then discovering the asset we mortgaged has lost its value by the time we've paid off the loan. Many times by the time we reach the top of the corporate ladder and think we now have time to spend with our families they've already grown up and left. We think we'll work extra-long hours so we can take an early retirement, retire at 55, then discover we don't have a healthy body left to enjoy it and die of a heart attack at 58. That's much like working hard for 20 years to pay off a mortgage and then discovering the house is only worth a fraction of the price we paid for it because we neglected to maintain it because we were too busy paying for it. Sound ridiculous? Sure does, but that's how many people live their lives. That's the way I was living my life (success at any price, even if it meant failure at life). I was about to discover that passion without balance is the path to burnout.

SURPRiSe!

It all began with a terrorizing grip of anxiety as the last envelope was opened. The project was the biggest one I had ever attempted: a 97-home residential subdivision in the village of Plattsville, a far cry from the 16-unit apartment building and the 6 single-family homes I'd previously built. I'd already spent over $50,000 on engineering fees and had purchased the land. The bids we were opening that day, I thought, would give me an early glimpse of how much money I stood to make on the deal.

But as the township clerk, my engineer and I sat opening envelope after envelope in the council chambers of the township offices that sunny April afternoon in 1987, the prospect of personal financial ruin lunged out at me like a vicious tiger. It threatened to destroy all that I'd worked so hard for over the past five years.

The greatest troubles I ever had never happened.

BURNOUT

My heart palpitated wildly and waves of anxiety pulsed through me, a reaction unlike any other I'd ever experienced. I was scared, not only about the business but also by the unfamiliarity of fear itself.

That night in bed, my mind raced as my body tossed around trying to shake the mental agony I was experiencing. This guy who was once so passionate about life, so positive and so full of energy, could now find potential disasters lurking in almost every deal I was involved in. My body was drenched in a cold sweat, and I didn't get more than an hour of sleep that night.

Morning failed to bring any relief at all. Normally I'd get out of bed and hit the floor running. That morning, however, I dreaded facing the day. Pulling myself off the bed, I made it as far as the couch before collapsing. My wife Elizabeth wanted to know what was wrong, but I wasn't sure. I could only tell her about the anxieties that had coursed through my head during the night, the pains I was feeling in my chest and the difficulty I was having with my breathing. It was as if everything broke down at once.

When I did summon up the energy to go to work, all I could do was walk into my office, shut the door, put my head on my desk and cry. I accomplished very little that morning, and when I went home for lunch, I broke down again. After forcing myself to eat some lunch, I ended up crawling into bed and slept for a couple of hours.

HELL ON EARTH

As much as I desperately wanted the emotions of the first two days to fade, it seemed there was nothing I could do to alter my feelings. Worse still, they didn't disappear when I went to bed that night. They were there the next day...and the next...and the next. For the next four months I went to hell and back so many times I could conduct tours.

From May to August I battled depression, anxiety, despair and lethargy. I went through the motions at work, and found myself having to build up energy for even the smallest job. Trying to camouflage my feelings in front of others, I faced a daily struggle to say the "good mornings," give the pep talks and be the team leader that everyone expects of the company president. Today, I know that going to work ultimately helped me recover, but at the time I was constantly tempted to let the business slide. I just didn't care.

It wasn't much easier at home. My children wanted to play in the evenings, but after an exhausting day battling my emotions at the office, all I could do was lie on the couch, bury my head under a pillow and let my head spin. The noise they made drove me crazy, but they were just kids having fun. I was in no mood for fun. Everything was more difficult. Dragging myself out of bed in the mornings was a chore. Obstacles that I would have steamrollered before now seemed insurmountable.

I dreaded decisions that in the past I would have made virtually without thinking. The contractor's bids had ignited my burnout, but they weren't what was keeping my spirit in intensive care. In fact, the development deal had turned out much better than originally expected (I actually ended up making a lot of money on the project). The crisis surrounding the deal had merely brought to light much deeper problems.

The worst times were when I was alone, especially on drives between work and home or between the office and a project. Alone in the car with my thoughts, I would at times consider ending it all. My greatest fear was that I'd never get better. Furthermore, it was clear that the business success I'd counted on to give me happiness had ultimately brought me misery. My passion for life was gone. Life had lost its meaning. Driving along the road, I often considered ramming my car into the closest solid object.

HeLP!

What I really longed for, was someone to explain to me what I was going through, but it seemed nobody could. Well-meaning friends advised me to cut back on the stress in my life by selling the company. My wife advised me to pull myself up by the bootstraps and cut out the self-pity. Friends urged me to stop being so negative and

Ben KUBassek

down in the dumps, without realizing I had little control over how I felt. Even my doctor at first simply prescribed medication to calm my nerves and to help me sleep.

I had never thought about burnout. If I had heard the word, I hadn't known what people were talking about until, in September, my doctor informed me that what I was going through was total mental, physical and spiritual burnout. He ordered me to change activities and location immediately. The next day I left for Florida determined not to come back until I felt that I could no longer stay away. The two and half weeks our family spent relaxing on Daytona Beach were a time of introspection for me. I thought about all I had so passionately achieved over the past seven years. More importantly, I thought about the person I'd become and how I was feeling at the present time.

Fundamental changes were clearly in order, and the realizations I came to gave me hope that I could recover. Not only hope that I would recover and pull myself out of my debilitating state, but that I could ultimately beat burnout. I believed I'd found a formula for living that guaranteed I'd never burn out again. Doctors tell us that if we burn out once we have a 50 percent chance of it happening a second time. If it happens twice, there's a 70 percent chance of it happening a third time, they say. Not what my insurance company, or I, wanted to hear.

I wasn't over-committed, I was simply imbalanced.

Among other things, these realizations had to do with achieving balance in life, dealing with stress and achieving goals in ways that avoid burnout. The fact was, I wasn't over-committed, as people told me. In fact, I was uncommitted to my family, friends, fitness and faith. I was only committed to my finances. I wasn't over-committed, I was simply imbalanced.

I wasn't doing too many things. In fact there were a whole lot of things that I was not doing. Things with my family, my friends, my fitness (mentally *and* physically) and my faith. I wasn't doing too many things, I was just out of balance. The stress of living without balance had almost been enough to destroy me.

STRESS—THE INVISIBLE EPIDEMIC

We live in a high-pressure world. Everyone seems to be demanding a lot more from us. Our bosses expect us to do more with fewer resources and in less time. We master one new technology and two more are on the market. Our customers are more demanding than ever before. The constant changes in the marketplace are overwhelming. Information, information, information. We can't handle any more! The epidemic being created by these challenges (which is almost invisible but deadly just the same) is called stress.

The only way to master stress and avoid burnout is to find a better way to live. A way of living that embraces change and allows us to experience the joy of Real Living. Living in total abundance and Real Prosperity. A life where we "don't sweat the small stuff." A life where we no longer carry stuff (like unforgiveness) that's been dragging us down and sapping our energy. A life that is lived in congruence with our beliefs. Where we walk our talk. A life where there is Real Balance, integrity and harmony. A life that makes a difference, a difference in the home, in the office, on the job, in the community and around the world. A life of joy, peace and love. Sound too good to be true? It's not. It's the abundant life you and I were born to live. The key is to learn to really live, before it's time to die. If we love our kids enough to die for them, why don't we love them enough to live for them?

We have heard enough about change over the past 10 years to make us all sick of the word. Therefore, I'll try to refrain from the use of the word as much as possible for the rest of this book. We'll focus on the positive: Finding a better way. You may wonder how we could possibly find a better way to live when we can't seem to find the time for everything we are presently doing. There is a way, but before we look at how, let's spend some time trying to understand why we may need to find a better way to live. Why we need to find Real Balance (a balance between family, friends, fitness, finances and faith. The reason these five "F" words are so important is the fact that we are all created with six basic human needs. These five "F" words are the aspects of life that are designed to meet those needs. That's their purpose.

If the human needs within us go unmet, we pay a price with our health, our happiness, our relationships, our families and our finances.

As human beings we are all created with the same 24 hours in a day and the same basic human needs. If the human needs within us go unmet we pay a price with our health, our happiness, our relationships, our families and our finances. These needs are as real as the need for food and water but not as obvious. They only become obvious when unmet, much as we only realize we have a need for food when we get hungry, and we only realize we have a need for water when we get thirsty.

Most people have bodies and relationships that are crying out the symptoms of stress and imbalance, which means some needs are not being met. But we carry on with our lifestyle, thinking that somehow things will get better. So we just try harder, get more positive, get more efficient, and we're still not meeting our needs. It's like being thirsty and eating another donut instead of taking a drink of water. Understanding our needs is the first step toward taking action to meet those needs.

Just as being thirsty is a warning sign of dehydration and hunger is a warning sign of starvation, there are warning signals for all human needs in our bodies. If we never experienced hunger we'd die of starvation. If we never experienced thirst we'd die of dehydration. There are other warning signals that can prevent premature death physically, mentally and spiritually, if we only knew how to interpret them and take action to meet the need at hand (just as being thirsty signals dehydration and we take action to meet our need for water by taking a drink). Let's look at our human needs one at a time, what they mean to us, what warning signals will appear if the need goes unmet, and how we can meet that need in our lives.

Guarantee

We are all created with a need for guarantee, or consistency, or security (whatever you want to call it). Even though we all have this need, some of us have a greater need for it than others do. Obviously, I have a lot less need for guarantee than most people do. I've never had a paycheck that I've not personally signed. I wouldn't want it any other way. I'm an entrepreneur who doesn't know why he has a Registered Retirement Savings Plan because he never plans to retire. I have so much fun in business I don't want to quit just because I reach a set age.

It's self-worth that determines net worth in the end.

We all know about the downsizing and rightsizing that is happening in North America. There are many people being pushed into entrepreneurship whether they are cut out for it or not. As Michael Gerber says in his book *The E-Myth*, "most entrepreneurs are just technicians having an entrepreneurial seizure." This can be very stressful for many people. A joint venture can be the answer. Or perhaps you form a strategic alliance with your former employer to provide your services on contract. The key is to be prepared for whatever may lie ahead by practicing growth on a daily basis. Your employer is focused on your achievements. However, you must focus on the person you are becoming in the process, and you will never have to worry about the future. You will have such tremendous self-worth that you'll be confident you can handle whatever may come. It's self-worth that determines net worth in the end.

The one area where we all need stability, security and consistency is in the home. It really doesn't matter whether we are a successful executive, or a child, we all need the haven of rest called *home*. A place where there is peace, harmony and love. A shelter in the time of storm. This haven has become *hell* for many and we are all paying the price (some directly, others indirectly).

The destruction of the family unit that has taken place over the past 10 years or so has taken a tremendous toll on everything from corporate profits to the physical health of many employees. The stress created in the home is brought into the workplace. The kids take the stress created in the home to school. There, the teachers pay the price for our stupidity and self-centered actions.

So what are the warning signals that indicate there is a lack of guarantee in your life? See how you do answering the following questions:

1. Do you constantly worry about making ends meet?
2. Are you concerned about how much money you'll have to retire on?
3. Are you worried about what would happen to you financially if you lost your job?
4. Are you concerned about how you will fund the education of your children?
5. Do you worry about how your children will turn out?
6. How well are your children doing in school? Academically? Behaviorally? Socially?
7. Do you worry about your health?

If you've answered yes to any of these questions it could be an indicator that you are deficient in the area of guarantee. Not to worry. As we discover the power of Real Balance and the five "F" words, you'll see how your guarantee needs can be easily met in every area of your life.

GaMBLe

It almost seems like a paradox, but just as we have the need for guarantee and consistency, we also have the need in our lives for some gamble, some risk and some inconsistency. The key is balance, and to understand in which areas of life we need more guarantees, and in which areas we need more gamble. I personally have a small need for financial security but a great need for family security. I need to know that when I get home, they will *be* there to greet me. The security of a stable home is the foundation of success in all other areas of life.

It's not only important to understand our needs in these areas but also to understand the needs of our spouse and children. Sometimes entrepreneurs create a lot of stress in the home by not providing the assurance of security our families need. Corporate executives move at the request of the company and pull their kids out of their school and away from their friends without thinking about their needs. Pastors are terrible for this. They move their families from one church to the next, and from one parsonage to the next, without realizing their spouses may need the security of owning their own home. Likewise many times there is needless stress in the home because the stay-at-home spouse doesn't understand that their partner has a higher need for risk and inconsistency, and as a result withhold their support.

The need for risk is what drives the entrepreneur to achieve bigger and better things. One of my lawyers, Craig Robson, has said to me a number of times, "Why is it that every real estate developer seems to have a death wish?" He doesn't seem to understand it's not just the money, but the need to take risks, that fuels the fire. It's the excitement of making a decision in faith, not knowing the outcome but believing the venture will be successful. The greater our need for risk, the more exciting our lives are. The key for people with high-risk needs is to balance their need for risk with the high-security needs of people around them.

GROUP

John Donne said, "No man is an island unto himself." The need for people to be together has been around since the beginning of time. Just as there is no substitute for solitude in our everyday lives, there is no substitute for fellowship. Many people through history have tried to create community, especially during the hippie movement of the '60s. Few have had much success, other than the Hutterites in Western Canada and the American Midwest. The early church in the Book of Acts inspired my grandfather to create such a way of life, and the Hutterite colony was the model he followed. Having spent 21 years of my life in a commune, I can tell you there are many benefits to living in community. However, there are many other ways to meet the need each one of us has for fellowship.

Professional associations are a great place to meet people with the same profession or business interests. Service clubs are an excellent place to associate with people with same desire to serve the local community. Serving on the board of a charity or mission is a great place to network with other people who share your passion to change the world. Mastermind groups are an ideal place to network with like-minded individuals. A mastermind group is a group of like-minded individuals who meet regularly to empower, encourage and challenge each other. Usually a group of four to six people works the best. It's a forum where each person can share their victories, their challenges and their hurts, knowing everyone in the group loves them unconditionally and wants to see them win.

Church is a fantastic place to fellowship with others who share your beliefs. It can be a wonderful time of coming together with friends in an atmosphere of worship, gratitude and praise. A time of inspiration and motivation with like-minded people who wish to grow in their faith.

GOOD ENOUGH

I firmly believe that every human has a need within to know they have value, that they are making a difference, that they have significance, that they are good enough. I also believe that even though we are all born to win, most of us have been programmed as children to fail. Our parents, based on their own self-limiting thinking, programmed our subconscious to think the same way. It was the way they spoke to us. It was their actions that spoke even louder than their words.

I'm thankful for parents who believed in me and had extremely high expectations of me to achieve excellence in whatever I chose to do. I knew from the time I was a child I had a purpose here on earth. Living up to those expectations created some challenges for me, but all in all they made me a bigger, better person. Children need to know we believe in them, we're proud of them, we love them. Not only do they need love, they need structure as well. They need rules to measure themselves against, to give them a sense of accomplishment and fulfillment when they do measure up.

Many adults I meet on a daily basis and in my seminars have a very low sense of selfworth and significance. They don't feel as if they are making a difference. I've seen these people's lives drastically changed after they take a mission trip or a "volunteer vacation," as Faith Popcorn refers to them in her book *Clicking*. My first mission trip in 1992 was one of the most life-changing experiences of my life. Many people who read my first book *Succeed Without Burnout* and took my advice to go on a volunteer vacation have told me it has changed their lives. Whatever your skills are, they can be used to make the world a better place if you just take the first step. Sign up for a construction or medical team going to a Third World country. Giving into the life of a less fortunate soul will give you a whole new sense of purpose and self-worth.

GROW

The need to grow and move to higher levels in all areas of life is a need as great as our need for food. Without growth, we die. Without a daily diet of positive life-changing information being fed into our brains, they shrivel up. That daily diet can be reading or listening to teaching tapes while you commute. As we start feeding our minds with this information we begin to grow mentally and increase financially. We get better at our relationships and our faith begins to build. Success breeds success. As we begin to grow we begin to fathom our potential, and at that point the sky is the limit.

Just as we need to grow mentally, we need to grow spiritually or we die spiritually. More on that later. It has little to do with religion. We are simply spiritual beings having a physical experience and we can't understand Real Balance if we don't understand the spiritual side of ourselves.

We also need to grow financially. If you already have all the money you need, set increased goals in the area of your giving. If a business isn't growing it's dying. If we're not growing our personal finances we are dying financially. The same is true physically. If we stop growing new skin, new blood cells and fingernails, think how quickly our bodies would die. If we stop growing new hair we go bald; just ask me. Whoever said "hair is a renewable resource" hasn't seen my hairline.

Give

The final human need we have is the need to *give*. This can mean giving time, money, encouragement, praise, love, hugs, whatever. Whatever you are giving out, you will get back. It is a natural cycle. It's a principle. What goes around comes around. Nevertheless, we all have a need to give. It's the way we plant seeds for the harvest we will one day reap. Giving to others takes the focus off our own problems. As we begin to look at creating Real Balance and controlling stress in our lives, we will see how helping others in need really does make our problems look much smaller and eliminates a lot of stress.

The human needs we have been born with exist whether we recognize them or not. The key to Real Prosperity is to find a way to live our life in Real Balance, making certain that every human need is met daily. The way to achieve that Real Balance is to come up with a plan for our lives that is personalized for us. One that focuses on and meets our needs and the needs of our family. It is critical for us to follow our own dream, not someone else's. I call this personal plan the Five "F" Words to Real Balance.

THE FiVE "F" WORDS

The first F represents our need for **Fitness**—balancing our need for both physical and mental growth and exercise and our need for rest and relaxation.

The second F stands for the **Family** and our need to balance providing for, spending time with, and building a successful family.

The third F represents our **Friends** or our social life and the importance of balancing our human need to be part of a group and spend time in solitude with our best friend—ourselves.

The fourth F reminds us of the area of **Finances** and our need to be balanced between earning, spending, saving and giving.

The fifth F stands for **Faith**—our need to believe in ourselves (self-esteem) and our need to balance that faith in ourselves with a faith in our Creator.

Yes, when you align these five elements properly, applying the principle of the law of the harvest ("whatever you sow you will reap"), you have achieved Real Balance and are well on your way to banishing burnout and succeeding in every area of life. This is Total Prosperity. However, as you will see, there is also a balance within each F that needs to be achieved. In the following chapters we will look at each "F" word and discover what Real Balance would feel like in that area. We'll look at how to find that balance for ourselves, and then keep that balance.

> **"Wisdom is knowing what to do next, virtue is doing it."**
> David Starr Jordan (1851-1931)

Part Two: The Five "F" Words

"Balance is less about striving for an elusive state of equilibrium than it is about making a series of choices in your life. You have to figure out what's important to you, and that's what will dictate how you spend your time....There's nothing easy about choices. But here's how I look at it: Either you make them for yourself, or they are made for you."

Dawn Gould Lepore

Fitness—If You Don't Feel Good, What Else Matters?

You can be fit without being balanced but...you can't be balanced without being fit.

When I'm speaking in my seminars across the country the most common question I'm asked is: "Where do I start in my quest for life balance?" My answer is always: "If you don't feel well, what else matters?" Start working on your fitness. Think about it. If you're sick in your body or your mind, every other aspect of life is affected. Good health is something many people would give millions to acquire, if only it could be purchased with money. The truth is, billions of dollars are spent every year in North America in an attempt to treat the symptoms of our sick society. Unfortunately, most of those dollars are spent on disease treatment instead of health care.

Generally, people who don't feel well want to get better immediately. You can live without your family, without your friends, even without your money. You can't live without your health. Health is one of those things we take for granted as long as we think we have it, and become enormously concerned about it as soon as we think we're going to lose it.

The public in general believes they are healthy if they are not experiencing symptoms of illness. However, the absence of symptoms doesn't necessarily mean we are experiencing health. Disease is usually present in our bodies long before the symptoms show up. You can be free of symptoms and have a stroke or heart attack tomorrow. The presence of disease is the harvest we reap from sowing the seeds of an unfit life. Our bodies have been created to live in harmony, integrity and balance. Living a life of mental and physical fitness will result in a harvest of wellness. By focusing on what our human needs are instead of the things that are bad for us and we need to quit doing, we can achieve balance much more quickly.

Mention the word fitness and most people conjure up the image of hulking figures pumping iron, or competing in triathlons, or simply jogging at the neighborhood Y. Granted, physical fitness is extremely important, but when I talk about fitness being important to keeping our lives in balance, I'm speaking of several different types of fitness. They include mental, physical and emotional (spiritual) fitness, since humans are tri-dimensional. Fitness is a combination of strength, endurance and flexibility. To be fit we need a balance between all three.

There is a connection between our mind, body and spirit. The thoughts we sow in our mind will affect our physical well-being. The way we look after our physical body will determine our emotional (spiritual) well-being. In each area we are what we are because of the seeds we have sown (seeds we have sown in our mind, in our body and in our spirit). We always reap what we sow. The seeds we've planted are the causes of our disease; the symptoms we experience are simply the harvest. Don't treat your harvest—plant a different seed.

Mental Fitness

An average adult thinks about 60,000 thoughts per day. It is our thoughts that lead to our actions. We can be totally transformed by renewing our minds. In order to renew our minds we must focus on that which is good and pure and pour those things into our minds until that which occupied it previously is diluted and eventually replaced with the new. Whatever we focus on gets bigger. Likewise, if we focus on those things we don't want, they also increase. The condition of our minds is determined by the diet we feed our brains, just as the shape of bodies is determined by the diet we feed our stomachs. Just like our bodies, our minds require exercise and rest as well as nutrition in order to grow and maintain fitness.

Mental nutrition is the food you feed your mind. As soon as you wake up in the morning, begin feeding your mind with positive life-changing information. Information fed to the mind within 15 minutes of awakening is digested very quickly and efficiently. Just as you have a dining room to feed your body, you need a dining room to feed your mind. A place of solitude where you go every morning as soon as you awake. My place is my reclining chair in the family room. That is where I spend 30-45 minutes feeding my mind during my Power Hour. I also feed my mind as I drive, by listening to motivational tapes.

LiGHten up

"If you're not having fun you're not doing it right" is a line I've used for many years. If I'm working at a project or spending time with my family and I start to get uptight or stressed out, I say to myself "Ben, you're not having fun any more. You're not doing this right." It forces me back to living in the present. Forget about how happy you'll be after you've gone through this crisis, or after you've reached some goal—perhaps paid off the mortgage or accumulated a retirement nest egg. You may not live another week, let alone another year. Learn to put some humor into everything that you do and especially into everything that happens to you.

There are many situations in which a little humor can help us calm down and allow us to make a rational judgment. Jerry Lee Lewis says the best wedding gift he received was a videotape of the entire ceremony. When things would get rough in the early days of that marriage, he would go into a room by himself, play the tape backwards, and walk out a free man.

If you don't like some of the signs of aging that are showing up, or some physical feature God has blessed you with that you wish He hadn't, make a joke about it. Have fun with it. My buddy Wayne, who has lost all the hair off the top of his head, is as shiny as a billiard ball. Wayne doesn't seem to mind. One year for Halloween he put on a turtleneck sweater, rolled it up over his ears, covered his scalp with baby oil, and went around as a roll-on deodorant. Relax and have fun; you may only have a few minutes left. You don't lose much hair after you're dead.

Have fun with whatever is happening to you. Learning to laugh at yourself is really important. You then stop taking yourself so seriously and start having a little laughter in your life. What an excellent and easy way to control your reaction to the stress you face every day.

"There are three things which are real:
God, human folly, and laughter.
The first two are beyond our comprehension.
So we must do what we can with the third."
John F. Kennedy

Take your job seriously...and take yourself lightly. You can be serious without being solemn. In a recent survey of 737 CEOs, 98 percent said they would much rather hire somebody with a good sense of humor than somebody without one. In the words of Don Seibert, former CEO and chairman of the JC Penney Company:

The most senior people and virtually all of the chief executive officers with whom I'm personally acquainted have highly developed senses of humor. Humor is a common thread I've seen in thousands of meetings in different companies on the most serious of subjects. Humor helps you keep your head clear when you're dealing with the most highly technical information or difficult decisions where choices aren't that clear.

HUMOR JEST FOR HEALTH'S SAKE

Without your health, you're dead. Humor not only keeps you living longer but lets you have a lot more fun while you're at it. According to William Fry, Jr., M.D., who has done research on the physiology of laughter for 45 years, laughter is like "internal jogging." He says laughter enhances respiration and circulation, oxygenates the blood, suppresses the stress-related hormones in the brain and activates the immune system. It is also a powerful antidote for stress. Laughter is indeed the best medicine!

Six Steps to Better Mental and Emotional Health:
1. Accept the fact that you alone control your attitude. Determine to take control of yours today.
2. Evaluate everything you feed your mind, every book, movie, TV program and video. Before reading or viewing it ask the question, "Is this going to help me in my personal, family and business life?"
3. Expand your vocabulary. Learn one new word a day.
4. Read something every day that will inspire, motivate and educate you.
5. Listen to teaching and motivational recordings while you drive.
6. Select your inner circle with care. Those people you associate with have an impact on the type of person you will become.

> **"The doctor of the future will give no medicine but will interest his patients in the care of the human frame, in diet, and in the cause and prevention of disease."**
>
> Thomas A. Edison (1847-1931)

Fighting Fit

The second area of fitness that we're going to talk about is the area of physical fitness. Achieving physical fitness is about much more than simply getting regular exercise and eating a good diet. It's about nutrition, it's about sleep, it's about oxygen, it's about physical balance and it's about lifestyle. All in all, it's about achieving a state of total wellness.

Exercise

Exercise is not optional. Inactivity kills. It stagnates the brain and poisons the body. This is not some philosophical concept. It is scientific and medical fact. The fittest generally live the longest and are the healthiest.

Regular and moderate exercise offers many benefits: a feeling of well-being, increased self-confidence, reduced irritability and fatigue. Above all, research studies show that a person who exercises becomes noticeably healthier. The more physically active a person is the lower the risk of suffering a heart attack. Exercise can also help relieve anxiety and tension found in high-pressure work or in challenging life circumstances.

For weight control, exercise offers a double benefit: it not only uses up calories directly, but extra calories continue to be burned away by the body up to 15 hours after the exercise. In general, exercise decreases appetite, helping the body to readjust food intake to energy expenditure. With all the benefits of exercise, why are more people not doing it? I'll tell you why. Because it's easy to do and it's even easier not to do!

Dr. Kenneth Cooper says that when you exercise, you activate the pituitary gland, flooding the system with endorphins, which are two hundred times more powerful than morphine. As a result, for the next one to three hours, your energy level is higher and your creativity is at its peak.

Years ago Dr. Cooper began his intensive study of people who exercise. He discovered that there was a notable physical and medical improvement in people who maintain a regular exercise program.

However, he also found that if a person's exercise program was directed only at muscle building, the individual really never achieved real physical fitness. In his book *Aerobics* he explains that one of the great misconceptions in the field of exercise is the myth that muscular strength or agility means physical fitness.

COMING UP FOR AIR

The key to fitness, Dr. Cooper says, is *oxygen*. In the body the fuel is the food we eat, and the flame to burn the fuel is oxygen. The body can store food, but it can't store oxygen.

Most people can produce enough energy (oxygen in their blood) to perform ordinary daily activities. However, if their activities become more vigorous, thus requiring more energy, they can't keep up. They feel tired.

As you increase your oxygen capacity you increase your endurance and overall fitness. This spread, the difference between your minimum requirements and your maximum capacity, is the measure of your fitness.[3]

Dr. Cooper believes that he found the secret to effective exercising programs when he identified oxygen consumption as the key measuring device for fitness. He became famous as a result of measuring needed oxygen consumption of different types of exercises and developing the aerobic exercise program, which is used by thousands of people around the world. Dr. Cooper states that aerobics forces the body to consume increased amounts of oxygen, and this is the only form of exercise that benefits not just skeletal muscles, but the whole body.

Stress causes improper breathing and leads to lower productivity; practicing deep rhythmic breathing will increase energy and endurance levels. Many people don't realize they use their mouths to breathe. That's as bad as trying to drink a milkshake through your nose. The nose is designed to warm, filter and purify the air we take into our lungs. Also, be certain you are filling the bottom third of your lungs. The next time (hopefully not next month) you go for a walk or run, practice breathing through your nose. It's simple: four steps breathe in (filling your diaphragm), four steps hold it, and four steps exhale. It will take a while to get back to your original pace, but keep at it.

If you spend a lot of time indoors, even during a hospital stay, use an indoor ozone air purifier that adds oxygen to the air. Stress and junk foods rob the body of huge amounts of oxygen. Powerful natural herbs like Siberian ginseng help reduce body stress, eliminate brain fatigue and improve oxygen use. Also drink plenty of purified, oxygenated water.

Diet

In *Succeed Without Burnout* I spent a lot of time talking about "the laws of the harvest." These biblical principles are key to achieving Real Balance. Total wellness is a state we achieve, the person we've become, the harvest we are reaping in our bodies. In our bodies, as in all other areas of life, we reap what we sow, or in other words we become what we eat. If you don't like your weight, or body shape, or energy level, take a look at what you have been eating. More importantly, since we determined to stay focused on the positive, look at what you should be eating. Think about it—there are more fat-free foods available than ever and there are more fat people than ever. Eating a balanced diet is important if you want to live a balanced life.

Liz Pearson, author of *When In Doubt, Eat Broccoli*[4] says the 80/20 rule applies to diets. Eat right 80 percent of the time and don't worry about the other 20 percent. She says eat fruits and vegetables by the truckload. Here's a list of the top ten foods she recommends:

1. Berries
2. Broccoli
3. Cantaloupe
4. Carrots
5. Citrus Fruits

6. Leafy Dark Greens
7. Mango
8. Red and Green Peppers
9. Sweet Potatoes
10. Tomatoes

What we eat can cause cancer and heart disease starting at a very young age. I know. I had one uncle die of cancer at the age of 36 and another uncle die of a massive heart attack at the age of 38. Eat fish. Eating just two servings per week can lower your risk of heart disease by 50 percent. Eat smaller portions of meat and become a lean meat eater. Any meat with loin in the name is generally leaner meat. Have some meatless days. Eating nuts as a meat replacer can lower your risk of heart disease by 35 percent.

Pass the Beans

Get plenty of fiber. The average North American gets only 15 grams a day instead of the recommended 30 grams a day. Eat plenty of beans. My wife makes the greatest chili and bean salads. "They may create a little wind," says Liz, "but they sure are healthy." She even recommends a Toot Trap cushion that's very portable and can even go with you on your next flight. If you don't need it, you could always lend to the person seated next to you, should the need arise.

Eating is still better than starving;
- Eat early
- Eat often
- Eat balanced
- Eat lean

You can eat right without being balanced, but you can't be balanced without eating right.

Drink Up

What we drink is just as important as what we eat. Again, often it's what we're not drinking that's killing us. In human beings, 70 percent of the weight and 80 percent of the brain is water. Water, often called the "silent nutrient" is often overlooked or taken for granted. Yet, next to oxygen, water is the nutrient most needed for life to be maintained. You could live for a month without food but only a few days without water. Thirst is an indicator of a water shortage in our bodies. However, we actually begin dehydrating long before we feel thirst.

Water acts as a solvent, coolant, lubricant and transport agent. If you're inactive, your body loses up to 80 ounces of water a day— mainly in urine, perspiration (even invisible perspiration) and bowel movements. Every time you exhale, for example, you lose water vapor, adding up to one or two glasses a day. To replace this loss, you should consume at least six full glasses of water a day—a minimum of about 40 ounces. Of course, foods are 70 to 90 percent water, so don't count just glasses of water you drink in a day.

Water needs vary, depending on climate and activity. For example, intense exercise in hot, humid weather can cause excess water loss of a quart or more an hour through perspiration. That water must be replenished immediately to prevent serious dehydration, even death. If too much fluid is lost through sweating, blood pressure falls and decreases oxygen delivery to the brain. In addition, blood thickens and can't reach small blood vessels, while sodium and other vital electrolytes are depleted, threatening the body's sensitive chemical and electrical systems. Make sure you're getting your daily fluid quota of six to eight glasses of pure water.

Thirst is not always a good indicator of our body's need for water. So it's important to drink regularly, even if you don't feel thirsty. Drink a glass of water 30 minutes and again 10 minutes before an exercise. And remember to drink as much as you can immediately after. Caffeine is not a good source of water, since it actually dehydrates our bodies. Moderate doses of caffeine, or the equivalent of up to three cups of coffee a day, are considered safe for most people provided two cups of water are drunk for every cup of coffee.

The most incredible book I've read on this subject is *Your Body's Many Cries for Water.*[5] It's written by a medical doctor who has cured thousands of patients by re-hydrating them. By getting them to drink enough water, he has cured everything from ulcers to bladder stones to obesity. Keep a water bottle with you at all times, at your desk, when you exercise or when you travel.

A Little Wine Can Be Divine

There's good news for people who like to enjoy a glass of wine on occasion. Evidence is mounting about the positive effects of moderate wine drinking. Recently in *Asia Week* magazine experts testified that moderate wine may prevent maladies as serious as brain disorders, as well as most cancers.

R. Curtis Ellison, an epidemiologist at Boston University, conducted a study on non-drinkers who started having two drinks daily, equivalent to 30 grams of pure alcohol, reducing their risk of coronary heart disease by 28 percent. He is a firm believer in the "French paradox"—French people eat plenty of heart-clogging saturated fat, exercise very little and still have one of the lowest rates of heart disease in the world. But they drink lots of wine.

If you are allergic to alcohol or genetically predisposed to alcoholism, don't touch the stuff. Many religions consider alcohol taboo. I personally enjoy a glass of wine before dinner. At the commune I was raised in, we were taught to have moderation in all things. I thank God for a father who is a wine maker from way back. He taught me the meaning of moderation as young boy. I've never seen my father drink more than one glass of wine in a day. Never have I seen him drunk, or even close, for that matter. That's the model I strive to be for my sons.

The Drug of Choice—Caffeine

Few people know the harmful results of drinking seemingly innocent beverages that contain caffeine. Millions of people around the world make caffeine their "drug of choice."

The effects of caffeine can begin with as little as 60-100 mg.—the amount found in one cup of coffee.[6] The following is a list of popular beverages and their caffeine content per 6-oz. serving.

```
Coffee . . . . . . . . . . . . . . . . . .120 mg.
Tea  . . . . . . . . . . . . . . . . . . .100 mg.
Coca-Cola . . . . . . . . . . . . . . .40 mg.
Dr. Pepper  . . . . . . . . . . . . . .38 mg.
Pepsi Cola  . . . . . . . . . . . . . .36 mg.
Decaffeinated coffee  . . . . . . .18 mg.
```

Studies show that five or more cups of coffee a day increase the risk of heart attack by two and a half times.[7] Caffeine also increases the heart's need for oxygen, thus promoting cardiac muscle ischemia and irregular heartbeats.[8] It also has been shown to cause bladder and colorectal cancer.[9] It has also been tracked to cancers of the urinary tract.[10] Stroke is the third major fatal disease that is assisted by caffeine because of its cholesterol-elevating role. Caffeine also aids in constricting blood vessels.[11]

That cup of morning coffee raises blood sugar levels, and with its mind-stimulating action produces increased energy. While this may feel great, the elevated sugar levels trigger an insulin response that not only cancels this surge, but also produces a big "let down" within a few hours. Before you know it, you reach for another cup, and your moods start taking you on a roller-coaster ride—up and down, down and up.[12]

Caffeine over-stimulates the nervous system, thus tremors, nervousness, anxiety and inability to sleep are common results. "In time, these symptoms give way to chronic fatigue, lack of energy, and persistent insomnia."[13]

Five Steps to Kicking the Caffeine Habit

1. For the first five days of being caffeine-free, eat only non-stimulating simple foods such as whole-grain breads, fresh fruits and vegetables. Avoid stimulating foods such as peppers, spices, vinegar and refined sugar products. Also cut out the tobacco. These prolong your craving for caffeine and weaken your self-control.

2. Drink 6-8 glasses of pure water a day. If you don't like the taste just add frozen juice ice cubes or a slice of fresh fruit.
3. Take a shower using a stimulating shower gel instead of soap.
4. Drink natural herb tea as a pleasant alternative.
5. Develop an exercise program, preferably outdoors.

Sweet Dreams

Our energy is a renewable resource, but that means we need to be recharged from time to time. Think about your car battery and how often it would start the engine in your car if it were never recharged. When it comes to recharging ourselves, the key is rest. Adequate, efficient, restful sleep is as important as exercise and diet in combating stress, is absolutely essential for recovery from a burnout experience and is a critical component of a balanced life. Sleep deprivation is costing the corporate sector a ton of money and is starting to get some wide-eyed attention. Think of the space shuttle Challenger, The Exxon Valdez, Three Mile Island. All were serious disasters linked in part to human error caused by a lack of sleep.

Sleep expert Dr. Adam Moscovitch says we now sleep 20 percent less than our ancestors at the turn of the century. He says, "Sleep is not a waste of time. It's an important part of the body and mind's restorative process." Though increased automation and advanced technology have revolutionized the workplace and driven up profits, it is the employees who are ultimately paying the price. Struggling to balance demands of changing work schedules, family responsibilities and business travel has caused workers to develop depression, increased workplace accidents and even escalated drug abuse, he explains.

In his book *Power Sleep*, Dr. James Maas says in fact 50 percent of North Americans are chronically sleep-deprived and that we are a nation of walking zombies. He says, "We have got to drop this macho nonsense that it is great to get by with six hours of sleep per night. It is just plain stupid. If we want to have peak performers in the workplace, try adding one hour of sleep, which can increase alertness and productivity by 25 per cent."

I was shocked to read his statement since I've been a six-hour-a-night person for many years. I also said in *Succeed Without Burnout* that I believe most people sleep a half-hour too long every morning, and I am still convinced that rising at 5:00 a.m. is absolutely the most important step toward finding Real Balance. Getting more sleep means going to bed earlier, not sleeping later. Research has shown, that one hour of sleep before midnight is worth two hours after midnight. You may need to put a bullet through your TV if it's keeping you from getting to bed on time.

No News is Good News

The subconscious mind continues to work while we are asleep. In order to get a good night's sleep we must prepare ourselves for sleep. Working in the office till late at night or watching the eleven o'clock news is no way to prepare yourself for a refreshing sleep. Instead, you might wish to read a good book or relax in a bath just before crawling into bed. Perhaps you may even be fortunate enough to have someone give you a massage at bedtime.

Many people find that regular physical activity gives them an unexpected benefit: They sleep more soundly and wake up feeling more refreshed, in part due to increased amounts of deep sleep. Deep (phase 4) sleep is when the body restores itself physically, as opposed to R.E.M. (rapid eye movement) or dreaming sleep, which appears to have a more psychological function. Researchers have found that aerobic exercise, especially done in the afternoon or early evening, produces more deep sleep early in the night.

Exercise, even just a brisk walk or low-impact aerobics, can also help you get a better night's sleep in a number of indirect ways. The relaxation and muscle fatigue induced by exercise can overcome insomnia by making it easier to fall asleep and can extend sleep time by almost one hour, according to a recent Stanford University study of people with sleep complaints. By improving respiration, aerobic exercise can improve sleep apnea (obstructed breathing during sleep), the most common of all sleep disorders.

Exercise encourages weight loss, which helps reduce symptoms of sleep apnea and also may relieve depression, which is a factor for many people with insomnia. The benefits of exercise are especially important for older people, since exercise has been shown to increase the amount of sleep senior adults get per night and reduce the time it takes to fall asleep. But be sure you finish exercising 2 to 4 hours before bedtime—working out later than that can leave you too revved up to fall asleep easily.

Wake yourself up gently. Don't set your alarm clock to buzz loudly and startle you awake, but rather have soft music gently wake you. The same goes for your children. Don't go into their room yelling, "Get up or you'll be late for school." I go into their rooms singing "Good morning to you"; I rub their backs and say, "It's another great day. How about breakfast with Father?" It helps them start the day in a happy, positive mood. They arrive at school more relaxed and ready to learn.

WEEDLESS

Have you ever wondered why our country enforces laws against selling tobacco products to our youth, yet many adults enforcing the law are smoking themselves? Talk about confusing the poor kids! I guess what we're saying is, "Kids, smoking damages your health. It's not OK to start destroying your body until after you turn 18."

Smoking damages the heart by raising blood pressure, damaging blood vessels, promoting the buildup of fatty plaque in arteries and lowering levels of "good" HDL cholesterol, making the blood more likely to clot and depriving the heart of oxygen. If you smoke, quitting is the best thing you can do to prevent a heart attack.

Tobacco kills three times more Canadians than alcohol, AIDS, illicit drugs, suicide and murder all combined. Thirty years after science established cigarettes as a major cause of disease, the number of people dying from tobacco products continues to rise. That's more than forty thousand Canadians a year.[14]

Youth is not
a time of
life, it is
a state
of mind.

THE MAGIC OF HIGH TOUCH

In today's fast-paced world, we are all looking for ways to counter the stress of high-tech. One simple solution is called "high-touch" or "massage." In a society of "instant everything" we all seem to be running flat out at warp speed. Then the inevitable happens: Our bodies get sick to slow us down, and we wonder what happened. When we refer to sickness, we usually are referring to the symptoms we experience when we're sick, not the cause of our illness. The cause is usually lifestyle-related—living a stressful life.

Our bodies are able to heal themselves if given the time, space and environment to do so. One of the oldest and safest healing therapies for "Hurry Sickness," and for many other illnesses, is the healing touch of massage therapy. It is almost magical how the human touch is able to relax, soothe and heal. It should become a monthly ritual for every person.

Every living creature has a craving and a need to be touched. Touch is as important as food and water. Massage therapy acts as the perfect antidote for stress, while fulfilling our need for touch. Massage sends a message to the body to slow down and relax. With this relaxation comes a harmony, a sense of wholeness and inner peace. When we care enough for our bodies to spend the time and money to take care of them, it sends a message to our subconscious that we have value, and significance. How can others treat us with respect, if we don't respect ourselves? Get a massage. You deserve it. Besides, this is the only body you are going to get. Look after it.

Go for a chiropractic adjustment once a month, as well. Dr. Reinhart, my chiropractor, started to adjust my spine at the age of 15 after another kid in school shoved me down and threw out my back. I look forward to every visit. He is so positive, energetic and friendly. He's also a great philosopher. The last time I was there he spent 45 minutes giving me a treatment that I had received from other chiropractors in 45 seconds.

RecaPPinG

- Feed your mind as well as your body.
- Read at least two books every month.
- Listen to tapes when you drive.
- Lighten up, have more fun.
- Get at least one hour of sleep before midnight.
- Exercise regularly.
- Breathe deeply through your nose.
- Eat lean.
- Eat early.
- Eat often.
- Eat balanced.
- Drink at least five glasses of water daily.
- Drink less coffee.
- Get a massage once a month.
- Get a chiropractic treatment once a month.

FAMILY—SUCCEED AT HOME WITHOUT QUITTING YOUR CAREER

"Teach your children to remind you, 'But, Daddy, I'll only be young once!'"

Gary W. Fenchuk

One hundred and sixty eight hours in a week. Ten thousand and eighty minutes. It doesn't matter if you're Bill Gates or the Pope, that's the total number of hours God gives each one of us every seven days. And just like a regular paycheck needs to cover a host of bills, it never seems to stretch far enough. In today's busy families, we must learn to spend this resource wisely since it's the currency of the realm. "For several thousand years, mankind has used money as the primary means of establishing value," says researcher George Barna in *The Frog in the Kettle*. "While money will continue to play a major role in our decisions and actions, by the year 2000 we will have shifted to using *time* as our dominant indicator of value."

Since time is a limited resource, you will see how extremely important it is to spend it in the wisest manner possible. In a way that is balanced. Without balancing the use of our time it is impossible to achieve Real Balance. Even though some time choices are already made for us—we have to eat, sleep, work, commute (the home office trend is changing this for some), do the grocery shopping and groom our bodies—we all have some discretionary time to invest or simply spend.

Discretionary time is the same as discretionary money. Discretionary money is the money left over out of your paycheck after you've met all your previously committed obligations. Those are all the non-discretionary payments such as rent, mortgage payments, telephone, Internet access account, utilities, car payments, credit card payments, etc. Once you contract or commit to a financial obligation it is no longer discretionary. The same principle applies to time.

When we accept a job, assignment or project and commit to completing it in exchange for payment, the time we use to fulfill that commitment is non-discretionary time. So the normal definition of discretionary time has been the hours between the time we arrive home until we go to bed, plus the weekends. Since the corporation or our clients are the only ones we normally contract our time with, most of us consider all the rest of time as discretionary. Consequently our commitment goes to where the contractual obligations have been made.

What most people mean when they say "I'm so busy with my career or business lately, that I've no time for family or anything else" is that their obligation has become their priority. They have the time; it has simply become non-discretionary. So if there happens to be some time left between the time they arrive home from work and the time they go to bed, they have some discretionary time to spend with their family. Certainly, there must be a better way to live! Achieving Real Balance is impossible without a paradigm shift when it comes to the way we view our time and our ability to control the way we spend it.

Now this may sound crazy to you at first, but bear with me for a bit. I'm not talking about time management; we'll do that in the chapter on time management. What I'm referring to is *time commitment*. In other words, what we contract or commit our time to and not how efficiently we spend it. That comes later. Just suppose, for instance, that you signed a contract with your children to give them 10 percent of your time, or 16.8 hours a week, or 144 minutes a day. Most of us give 30 percent, or 50 hours a week, to our boss or our clients. Some a little more, some less. I'm saying, "what if we contracted just 10 percent out of the balance (the remaining 70 percent of our time) to our family?" Just 120 minutes during and immediately following dinner every evening and another 24 minutes to enjoy breakfast together. What we do with this block of time will have a profound effect on our children, our parents, our siblings and our marriage, if we still have one.

No Substitute For Parents

Nearly four out of ten children in America are being raised in homes without fathers and that soon may be six out of ten. It seems our culture has accepted the idea that fathers are not necessary in the "modern" family.

> "In 1960, the total number of children living in fatherless families was fewer than eight million. Today, the total has risen to twenty-four million."[15]
>
> The Christian Businessman

One out of every four children will live with a step-parent before the age of 16. If the present trend continues we will soon have more single-parent families than traditional two-parent, mom and dad families.[16] If you think these statistics are no big deal because kids are tough, read this letter a church pastor received from a third grade teacher living in midwestern USA.

I look at my seventeen students, and I feel a deep sadness. Out of these seventeen, only eight have both natural parents. Two of these watch dirty movies with their parents. One has been sexually abused by her brother.

Sally's mother walked out on her father and the two children when they were babies. When Sally was seven, she witnessed her father's death in an explosion near their home. She and her four-year-old brother live with a relative, who doesn't take the best care of them.

Amy's father was killed shortly after her mother remarried. Rosemary has no idea where her father is.

Peter's mother left town, and her husband has to raise the four boys alone. Peter started stealing last year to get attention. He said he missed his mom.

Barry's mother remarried. He hasn't seen his father in two years because he doesn't pay child support. Barry lives in another world.

Betsy gets to see her father when he visits their home. Her dad's new wife hates Betsy because she looks too much like her mother.

Bill has no idea who his father is. His mother is a lesbian. His grandmother raises him.

Andrea loves both her father and her mother. She wants to see them get back together. Her mother works at a tavern at night and takes the children there sometimes.

Bruce's mother has had three husbands. All have walked out on her. Bruce said his real daddy came back to see him one day. But he was gone two days later. I cried with him.

Last week, two other children had to transfer to another school. It seems that their mom and dad had separated.

It's little wonder our teachers are suffering from burnout. At school, the children who show up from dysfunctional and broken homes come with broken hearts and bring their pain with them to school. Children without love and structure in their homes suffer socially, mentally and intellectually. We are all a product of our environment. It is our environment that forms our beliefs, it's those beliefs that control our thoughts, those thoughts cause us to act and those actions determine our feelings. Instead of changing our environment we reach for drugs. I literally cried when I read the following story in our local newspaper:

'Happy Pill' Targets Kids

Prozac, the popular happy pill, may be targeted at stressed-out children now that its coverage of the adult market is almost complete.

The makers of this widely prescribed drug are seeking to market the drug to youngsters in peppermint and orange flavors.

North American doctors are increasingly turning to anti-depressants as a solution to the troubles of childhood. Prozac, now 10 years old, is already established as the '90s drug of choice for adults seeking to allay the stress of modern life. It is worth $1.73 billion US a year to its maker Eli Lilly.

Now a bottle of Prozac could take its place along side the Cheerios and pan-

cakes at the breakfast table.

There are well over 400,000 people under 18 in the US being treated with Prozac and the number of teenagers increased by nearly half in the last year. Among six to 12-year-olds, prescriptions rose by 298 percent.

The Record, August 18, 1997

Unless our homes improve, more third grade teachers will be writing letters and so will the teachers of all grades. It is sad when the people who have the most contact with our children, and are expected to educate, coach and prepare them for life in the real world, are no longer able to cope with the pressure they are under. Our children and our teachers are both paying for our stupidity as parents.

One BiG FaMilY

Big families were the norm when I was a child. My mother had 12 brothers and sisters and my father had 14. It was no wonder my dad and mom had 7 of us kids—a girl, then 5 boys and then another girl. Mom calls it a boy sandwich, and I came smack-dab in the middle. Until my youngest sister Rebecca came along, the 8 of us shared a two-bedroom apartment that was formerly used as a pigpen. Our pail-a-day sewage system was replaced eventually and we had running water.

The farm people believed that the Lord provided, providing... Providing we did our part, God would do his. If we planted the crop, fertilized, weeded it and cultivated it, God would give the increase or the harvest, and so we learned a work ethic and how to work hard at an early age. As we worked together on a project we would sing and have a great time making work fun for the whole team. We spent a lot of our summer holidays pulling weeds and picking rocks from the fields. We were taught that hard work was very important and that the sooner we learned how, the better.

I discovered that I quite enjoyed work and the long hours I was working. Many days I put in 14 hours for the same $1.00 allowance as everyone else. In the evenings after a long day we would go for walks and chat with each other for hours. We had no radio, TV or daily newspaper. We had to learn to communicate with each other or we'd be pretty bored.

So you see the farm was my family, my friends, my work, my *whole* life. Leaving it would be the biggest decision I'd face in my life. I was leaving my comfort zone to pursue a dream of a better life in the outside world. I was also leaving behind the girl of my dreams, my future wife Elizabeth.

success in Business...failure at life

I met Liz when her family joined the farm in 1967. I was only 9 at the time but old enough to know a good-looking girl when I saw one. By the time I was 15 I was secretly dating Liz. Secretly, because courtship was against the law at the farm. However, where there's a will, there's a way. When I left, I knew in my heart that someday Liz would follow and we'd be married. She did, and we did. A year after I left, I proposed to Liz; she accepted and left the farm. We were married that June. Since then God has blessed us with four beautiful children: Krystal, Daniel, Joshua and Jonathan.

To the outside world we looked like the ideal family. Not! I was spending more time with the business and less time with my family. I justified the longer hours by telling myself and others that I needed to provide for my family the good things in life I didn't have when I was growing up. What I didn't realize is that kids only remember two things when they grow up, which were of utmost importance to them as children. It's not how many things you bought them or how big your business was or how many employees their dad had. The things they remember are:

1. How much time they spent with their parents. Especially, how much time did dad take just to be with them? To play catch, to take them to their baseball games.
2. How much love was in the home? How much did mom and dad love each other? How much did mom and dad love the kids? Did they get lots of hugs and kisses? Lots of "I love you'" and "I am proud of you"? Did dad take the time to kneel down beside

my bed every night, put his face against mine and say a prayer of blessing over me?

Think about those two things: How much time they spend with their parents and how much love was in the home, and then think about the state of a family in today's society. More importantly, think about your family, think about my family and think about the law of the harvest. I was spending so much time at the office and so little time at home, and when I was home in body, my mind was still in the office. The seeds I was planting had no resemblance to the crop I wanted to reap.

Fortunately, I had a wife who was content to stay at home and raise the family, cook the meals, look after the garden and even mow our 5-acre front lawn. Reminds me of a story:

Brenda, pregnant with her first child, was paying a visit to her obstetrician's office. When the exam was over, she shyly began, "My husband wants me to ask you..." "I know, I know," the doctor said, placing a reassuring hand on her shoulder. "I get asked that all the time. Sex is fine until late in the pregnancy."

"No, that's not it at all," Brenda confessed. "He wants to know if I can still mow the lawn."

"Success in marriage is more than finding the right person: it is being the right person."
Robert Browning (1812-1889)

Well, I thought we had a great partnership. My wife had different feelings. I was busy building the business and she was busy building the family. She wished I would spend more time at home. I didn't listen. I didn't realize God designed family building teams to be husband and wife. It doesn't work as well any other way.

Unfortunately my attitude toward the family and the value I placed on it carried through to my business. I hired employees who spent less time with families when asked to spend more time at the office. I also hired burnout-prone people. These were people who wouldn't let

Ben KUBassek

lack of experience, lack of education or lack of time stop them from accepting any challenge I gave them.

I didn't realize other executives were facing the same crisis, and some were actually doing something about it—like Tom Bloch. He was the CEO of H&R Block and left his $618,000 job to take on a $20,000 a year job as a teacher. He says he didn't want to come to the end of life and look back and realize he had the opportunity to make a difference in kids' lives and didn't. Before he quit his job as CEO he would sit at the dinner table processing his business day. His kids would talk to him and many times he didn't even hear what they were saying.

I was much like Tom Bloch, growing slowly away from my family. It didn't happen all at once. As I hit burnout—that time of turbulence in my life—I became more irritable at home, more reclusive and less willing to join in family activities. Ironically I believe it was my suicidal thoughts that actually motivated me to reverse the process, to become what I am today, a much-loved husband and father playing a huge role in the lives of my family.

I began to realize how selfish my suicidal thoughts were. Recovering from burnout and discovering the value of the family, I realized that I would have missed seeing my family grow up had I taken my own life. My death would have been relief to me at that time but tragedy to my family. My boys would have had to attend all their baseball games without me, they would have had to go to bed every night without me there to pray with them, to hug them and kiss them. Who would have taught them how to catch a baseball, how to ride a horse? Who would bring flowers for my daughter on her birthday?

THankSGiVinG

Three months ago as I was dressing early one morning, I walked to my dresser to get a pair of underwear. As I opened the top drawer I noticed, lying on top of the dresser, a sheet of paper folded in half with "Dad" written across it. I picked up the paper, unfolded it and found the following letter from my 11-year-old son, Joshua:

Oct. 7/98

Dear Dad,

*Thanks for the great time you've given me golfing, riding in your heli-
copter, and letting me buy a dirt bike. Remember when you took me golfing
in the summer and you showed me how to golf? What about the time you
took me fishing and taught me how? Thank you for teaching me how to play
baseball. Thanks for taking me up in your helicopter and flying me where I
wanted to go. Thanks for everything you taught me, like building your office,
and letting me help build your helicopter. I love you Dad.*

Dad's Helper,

Joshua

How could I ever forget that afternoon of golf, I wondered, as I
wiped the tears from my eyes? We were almost thrown off the golf
course because my youngest son Jonathan decided it would be easier
to hit the ball out of the sand trap if he first built a little sandcastle to
place it on. He thought we were there to have fun! He couldn't understand the concept of "serious recreation."

Later that on that same week I received a letter with the same date
from my oldest son, Daniel, 13. Here's how it went:

Oct. 7/98

Dear Dad,

*Thanks for all the things you've done for me and all the time you spend
with me. The time we spent working on the office meant a lot to me, but the
time we spent working on my dirt bike means even more to me. Thank you
for taking time on Sundays to go horseback riding with me. Your support
when you took me to my baseball games was very much appreciated. You
have supplied me with all the things I need like clothes, food, a house, but
most of all love!*

Your son,

Daniel

Those letters are both stuck to the wall in front of my desk so I see them every day. They will always remind me that the little things really do make a big difference, and that kids really do remember our love more than anything else. Kids are a product of their environment. Kids can only be happy if their parents are happy. Kids can only feel love if there is love in the home.

A couple of years ago, when my youngest son Jonathan was 8, he brought me to realize that it wasn't only suicide that can cause parents to miss out on their family's childhood.

It was a Saturday afternoon and I was in the hangar working on my helicopter. Jonathan was out there with me; he was working on his bicycle. As I walked from the tail rotor I was repairing over to the work bench, I walked right by my son who was kneeling on the floor beside his bike. He looked up at me and said, "Dad, I love you" and of course I replied, "I love you too, Jonathan." I got the tool I needed and went back to working on my helicopter. A few minutes later Jonathan spoke again and said, "Dad, I'm glad you're not divorced." Taken by surprise, I didn't respond to that comment. Not getting a reply, Jonathan spoke again. This time he asked the question, "Dad, do know why I'm glad you're not divorced?" With tears starting to come to my eyes I replied, "No, son, why are you glad I'm not divorced?" Here is his response. He said, "Cuz I wouldn't be as happy as I am. Because then I couldn't live with the best Mom and the best Dad in the whole world." What a warm feeling came over me! That's what I call payoff.

FaMiLY TiMe

First we're dying to get married. And then we're dying to have children. And then we're dying for our children to grow old enough so we don't need to hire a babysitter. And then we're dying for them to leave home. And then we're dying to retire. And then, when we're dying…we suddenly realize we forgot to live. We also realize we forgot to enjoy our children while we could.

Time with family is high priority time, most people would agree. Why then, I wonder, is it the most negotiable? I believe too many people just wish it would happen, when in reality it will only happen if we allow time for it to happen. What I have found absolutely necessary is to block out family time in my schedule just as I would any other meeting time. That way when it's time to be with them, I simply say, "I have an appointment." The same applies for family vacations. If you want to be sure to take them, block that time out for your family, or something else will take it. Making time for family is like many other things; it's easy to do, and just as easy not to do.

Joy is not joy without laughter, love is not love without loving.

The headline of a recent edition of *Fortune* magazine asked this question: "Is Your Family Wrecking Your Career?" The article said that at one time a family was not only an asset, but also a prerequisite to making it up the corporate ladder. Today, in most corporations, a family is considered a liability. It's OK to have your family's pictures on your desk, just don't let them cut into your billable hours.

What some of these corporations don't realize is that better homes make better employees. Better employees build better businesses. So we could say that better homes mean better businesses.

Kids need time and kids need love, but kids also have a need to know that they are special. Every human has a need for significance. The self-esteem of your child will soar with a simple "I'm proud of you" or "you're special." Driving around between construction projects one Saturday morning I had 8-year-old Jonathan sitting in the front seat beside me. It was our special time to be together, as he calls it. I looked over at him and I said "Jonathan, you're special." He said, "Dad, I know I'm special. You know how I know I'm special?" "How?" I asked. "Because of what I have," he replied "You know what I have, Dad?—I have your love."

PRaise

Praise is something children can never get enough of. They can never hear "I'm proud of you" enough times in one day. The payoff comes in terms of self-confidence as they begin to perform beyond their expectations, both academically and socially. My daughter Krystal graduated from Grade 8 a couple of years ago. At her graduation ceremony one of the teachers walked onto the platform and began reading the following speech.

Wagler Citizenship Award

The citizenship award is one of the most prestigious awards to receive. The staff considers the following criteria in the selection of the recipient. A student worthy of the honour must demonstrate effective interpersonal skills such as co-operation, friendliness, and respect for self and others. He or she shows pride in the school and community by making a strong commitment to the betterment of the school. The student has been involved in school activities and is a positive role model who has earned the respect of both peers and teachers. This person demonstrates a consistent effort to improve personal performance while encouraging others to do the same.

This year we had a difficult decision in choosing one student and thus a dual award will be given. It is indeed with pleasure that I am able to bestow this honor on behalf of all the staff on one of the recipients.

This student not only meets the outlined criteria but practices it every day. It is an integral part of her demeanor. The recipient has spent only one year in our Wilmot Senior School but has contributed a tremendous amount both in the classroom setting as well as to the total program of the school.

Academically, she is exemplary for her peers by her consistently strong work ethic. She is a very unselfish student who is never too busy to help another student who may need assistance and encouragement.

The same traits hold true in her interaction with teachers. Her expertise in organization earned her many tasks which had previously been organized only by staff members. In fact, some of us are thinking that perhaps it is a good thing that she is graduating, or we may be out of a job.

This student has been involved in the school band and has been a keen participant for her teams intramurally in Physical Education. She gives her best effort at all times. Her upbeat, positive attitude is one to be admired. I believe that in your life, your attitude determines your altitude.

If this is true, this young woman should reach the stars.

May I proudly present and may you, Krystal Kubassek, proudly receive this award.

Never have I been so proud and felt so good! I had goose bumps all over. At the same I was fighting back tears of joy. This was my beautiful, intelligent daughter. This was true joy! This was real success! I'll never forget that evening as I watched Krystal proudly walk onto the stage and accept her award and the whole room went wild with applause. I truly believe she will reach the stars!

"All the wonderful things in life are so simple that one is not aware of their wonder until they are beyond touch. Never have I felt the wonder and beauty and joy of life so keenly as now in my grief that Johnny is not here to enjoy them. Today, when I see parents impatient or tired or bored with their children, I wish I could say to them, "but they are alive, think of the wonder of that! They may be a care and a burden, but think, they are alive! You can touch them—what a miracle!"

Frances Gunther

Recapping

- Tell your children that you're proud of them (whatever age they may be).
- Eat dinner as a family every night.
- Hug regularly.
- Spend two minutes cheek-to-cheek with your child every day.
- Bring flowers for your spouse when he or she is not expecting them.
- Provide love and structure to your children.

FRieNDS—CReaTiNG a WiNNiNG iNNeR CiRCLe

What Is a Friend?

A friend is someone who is concerned with everything you do.

A friend is someone to call upon during good and bad times.

A friend is someone who understands everything you do.

A friend is someone who tells you the truth about yourself.

A friend is someone who knows what you are going through at all times.

A friend is someone who does not compete with you.

A friend is someone who is genuinely happy for you when things go well.

A friend is someone who tries to cheer you up when things don't go well.

A friend is an extension of yourself without which you are not complete.

S. Shultz

Within every human being lies the need for fellowship, the need for affection and a need to be part of a group. Not just any group, but a group of like-minded people. People who have similar values, or values that we admire in all five areas of life. The first church in Acts was a group of people who shared the same values, the same beliefs and had all things in common. Since then there have been literally millions of church groups, associations and clubs formed for the purpose of bringing like-minded people together. Everything from motorcycle clubs to bird-watching clubs. From church groups to community service groups. From industry associations to the Society of Association Executives. There is an association for everything. Associations, clubs and groups are great, but that's not where we as humans begin building our friendships.

From early childhood on, we are all in need of love in order to live a balanced life. Our need for love does not diminish with age, but actually becomes a key ingredient of a healthy self-esteem as we become adults. Without love, our life is hollow and echoes with emptiness. With it, our life vibrates with warmth and meaning. Love makes the difference between living and breathing. Only when we learn to love, can we learn to live.

As a child we make friends with our classmates, the children in our Sunday School class and the other kids on our baseball team. As we move into our teen years, these same friends tend be the group from which we select our inner circle. If you want to know where your children are heading in life, check out their friends. Everyone knows that "birds of a feather flock together" but what not many realize is "they're all headed to the same place." Help your children select their friends and explain to them why you care about how they choose them. The friends our children choose will determine the heights they achieve in life. Our friends are part of our environment, and it is our environment that forms our beliefs as we mature.

However, as we go through life, friends will come and friends will go. As we move into our twenties and start building families, we get busier and find we have less time for our old friends. Our spouses and children many times fill the role of both family and friends. But to all things there is a season, and the family building season in our lives also comes to an end at some point in time. Quicker than most people realize, I'm told. If we rely only on our family to meet the need of friendship, the "empty nest" experience can find us lonely and without friends. Here's when many people die of loneliness. The need for friends changes as we move along our journey of life, but it's always there.

Why? What's the big deal about belonging to a group? Why do we need each other? Why can't we just go it alone and be happy and feel fulfilled? Well, remember the list of needs we're all born with. Friendship and fellowship meet almost every one of those needs to some degree. First there's our need for guarantee, some consistency and assurance that in the time of need there is someone we can call on. With fellowship and a close group of friends, or an inner circle, there comes a lot of opportunities to help each other. Helping each other, even if it's only moral support, helps meet another need every one has within them—the need for significance, to know in our hearts that we are making a positive contribution to someone else's life through our friendship.

WHO Cares

The encouragement we can receive from each other is often what it takes to get through a tough time we may be experiencing in our personal lives. Many times a friend's encouragement has prevented someone from committing suicide. Giving encouragement and praise also meets our need to give. I have a friend, Jim, who's the greatest encourager I've ever met. He calls me to tell me how great I am and what an excellent father I am to my children. He goes on and on. Boy, after I'm through talking to him, I feel like taking on the world. Those are the kinds of people I've chosen for my inner circle. The ones who make me feel better about myself and challenged to go a higher level as a result of being in their presence. It's amazing what the right friends will do for you.

Author John Mason says, "My choice to change my closest friends was a turning point in my life."

Dexter Yager, entrepreneur extraordinaire, says, "To be a winner you must associate with winners." He ought to know!

General Norman Scharzkopf said, "Your accomplishments do not make you great, it's your friends."

Robert Louis Stevenson spoke often about the value of friends, saying "a friend is a present you give yourself" and "friends are the end and the reward of life; they keep us worthy of ourselves." I am sure by now you're wondering, if friendship can be that rewarding, where do we find these friends and what do we look for in "inner circle" material?

HERE'S THE HOST OF OUR SHOW

When it comes to finding friends the law of giving applies. If you are looking for friendship, start to give friendship away. If you want a friend, be a friend. When you walk into a room filled with people, pretend you are the host. Don't wait for someone to introduce himself or herself to you. Imagine that it is your responsibility to make the other person feel relaxed and comfortable with you. Walk around the room and introduce yourself. Offer people a drink and they'll think you own the place. Be a host wherever go. Next time your association has a conference, offer to be the official hugger. Make people glad they have met you. Ninety percent of all people form that opinion in just a few seconds. In a meeting, networking event or presentation, you will be fully judged within the first four minutes. According to studies by Albert Mehrabian at UCLA, people's first impressions are based on three things:

55% —visual (how you look and act)

38% —vocal (how you use your voice)

7% —verbal (what you say)

Once you've properly introduced yourself, ask people about themselves. If it's a networking meeting, ask them about their business. Encourage conversation by asking open-ended questions like, "What's working?" or "How do you feel about that?"

People love to hear stories. Share an experience from your personal or professional life. Use humor. People would relax and enjoy themselves when they're around you, if you'd just lighten up. Set a goal to meet and keep two new contacts at each event you attend. As they hand you their business card, jot a personal note about them on the back of it. Be a mentor and offer to help someone with his or her business. At the same time be on the lookout for mentors. Make the most of every gathering you attend. It is the people we meet today that determine where we are tomorrow.

The power of association is a very powerful force in our lives. I have heard it said that **"we are the sum average of our inner circle, the five people that are the closest to us."** The people we associate with will determine the altitude we achieve in every area of lives—our families, our friends, our finances, our fitness and our faith. These people will also determine our attitude toward our family, friends, finances, fitness and faith. Our friends determine our future. We are all a product of our environment. If we want to change who we are, we must change our environment. Our environment can include our home, our car, our office, and yes, our friends.

So changing our environment may mean changing our friends. Or perhaps moving them from the inner circle to the outer circle. Changing friends is the toughest but usually the first step to changing our life. My friend Mark Victor Hansen says, "Find friends who have strengths you do not possess." Our friends can affect or limit our success in all five "F"s of life. We'll talk a little about each one and how their influences may be controlling us.

First, let's look at how our associations can affect our **family**. Hanging out with a bunch of guys who place little value on the family and would rather go out for a drink with the gang from the office after work than go home to be with their family will affect your attitude and the value you place on your family. Golf can rob a lot of family time until the kids are old enough to join you on the course. An inner circle of golf fanatics will affect your family life. BALANCE is the key when choosing your inner circle.

The area you'll really notice the power of associations is in the arena of your **finances**. People feel comfortable with other people that earn as much or less than they do. We have a tendency to associate with people who have accomplished less than we have financially. People who have accomplished less than we have make us feel more comfortable in our own state. Choose someone for your inner circle who is a real winner when it comes to finances. Someone who has a good track record of earning, investing and giving money. This person should be at a higher level than you in terms of income and net worth.

When it comes to our **fitness**, our associations do affect our attitude toward our bodies and what we are willing to accept as body weight and shape. Join a fitness club and you'll find people to make friends with who value a healthy body. Being in the company of physically fit people challenges us to keep ourselves fit. Find a mentally fit person as well for your inner circle. Someone who reads a lot, listens to motivational and educational recordings while they drive, and attends seminars regularly.

Finally, associating with people who are solid in their **faith** can help you soar to new heights spiritually. On the contrary, having people in your inner circle who do not attend church, never spend time in prayer or reading their Bible, will drag you down spiritually. Attending a dynamic, exciting place of worship is an excellent place to make friends to challenge you to new heights in your faith.

There are a number of places to find fellowship. Here's a recap:

- Church or synagogue is a great place to look if you're looking for friends or a mate with similar spiritual values.
- A service club is a good place to meet friends who are also interested in community service.
- Professional association meetings are a great place to meet people who share similar business interests. This is exceptionally true if you get involved on a committee.
- The Y or fitness club is an excellent place to find friends who will inspire you to keep your body physically fit.
- Organized sports such as baseball, soccer, hockey and basket-

ball are great places to meet other parents with children the same age as yours, and who are interested in investing some time in their family.

- A volunteer vacation with a construction team going to a Third World country to build a school, hospital or orphanage can be wonderful to make friends with people who share your desire to help the less fortunate and make a difference in our world.
- Network marketing groups have rallies where motivational speakers make presentations. These are usually great places to meet positive, upbeat people.

Don't Move!

Like all other valuable assets in life the asset of friendship also has its threats. For children, it can be the family move to accommodate dad's new promotion. Probably the greatest threat in my life has been my workaholic tendency. The way I was able to overcome this threat was to block time out of my schedule at the beginning of each month for fellowship. Time for church, time for entertaining and time for coffee or lunch with a friend.

In my experience, I have found it true that you have to be able to love yourself before you can love others. Develop integrity, honesty and character as the foundations for becoming a quality person and setting the stage for developing relationships with others. The more you focus on becoming (rather than just achieving), the more you will like the person you see in the mirror every morning.

Henry Drummond once said: "You will find when you look back on life that the moments when you have really lived, are the moments when you have done things in a spirit of love."

A healthy, balanced, successful person can be totally crushed by the withdrawal of love by a significant other. I personally know financially successful businesspeople and executives who were peak performers and took their spouse's love for granted. They acknowledged the supporting love of their spouse at home, giving them the self-confidence and self-esteem they needed to be super-achievers. However, they did not realize that their life partner wanted time, love and attention in return.

When these super-successful people discover that their spouse is leaving them, they are stunned. Many of them go into a state of depression, lose their appetite, cannot concentrate, have difficulty sleeping and begin to perform poorly on the job. Unfortunately, some even commit suicide.

Call Now

Sometimes a phone call is all it takes to keep in touch. It's a little thing that can mean so much! Call a friend right now. Someone you haven't spoken to in the past month. Ask them how they are. Heaven forbid, they might even tell you! Tell them that you appreciate their friendship. Tell them they make this world a better place. Think of something. Ask them if they need your help with anything. Or you may want to send an e-mail to say, "I'm thinking about you." It's free.

Flowers are also a great way to show your love and appreciation to someone. Send them flowers while they can still smell them.

A Blessing

Every day when I wake up I say, "Lord, make me a blessing to someone today." Like the song my brothers and I used to sing in our gospel quartet—"Lord, I want to be a blessing to someone today. Just a smile perhaps will do to help them on their way. To maybe lend a helping hand, or a kind word to say."

> "Beginning today, treat everyone you meet as if they were going to be dead by midnight. Extend to them all the care, kindness and understanding you can muster, and do it with no thought of any reward. Your life will never be the same again."
>
> Og Mandino

"The greatest bore in the world is the man who-- when you ask how he feels-- tells you."

seven secrets to great friendships

Have you ever wondered why some friendships you've had in the past have just fizzled before your eyes? People who were your best friends are like they don't even exist. That's because friendships need maintenance, just like all the other "F" words do. It's easy to start a fitness program or diet. It is much more difficult to maintain it. It is easier to make money than keep it. It's easy to make friends, but more challenging to keep them. Here are some ideas to help maintain and nurture your friendships:

1. Send five cards a week to friends and new acquaintances you've made in the past week. I buy generic wildlife cards by the case and use them for everything from birthdays to sympathy cards. Keep the message short, upbeat and encouraging.

2. Learn to accept people for who they are. Good friends give you the freedom to be yourself. Love others even if they're a little different. Give 12 hugs every day to people other than your family.

3. Look people in the eye. Have you ever noticed how little eye contact we have with strangers? Most of us aren't much better with our friends. Whenever hugging or shaking hands, always look the person in the eye as you release your grip.

4. Call three friends a week just to encourage them and find out

how they are doing. There is no better friendship booster than the ability to listen. The ability to show sincere interest is an admirable quality of a true friend.

5. Once a month, invite one of your friends for dinner. We have a few fondue pots and have a great time of fellowship, cooking our own food. It's a very relaxing way to eat and visit at the same time.

6. Forgive quickly. Lack of forgiveness is probably the number one destroyer of families and friendships. The Bible has an excellent formula to instruct us on when we should practice forgiveness and when we should not. It's simple. Only forgive others to the degree you wish to be forgiven yourself. No more. No less.

7. Be available. There is nothing like financial disaster or sickness to help us discover who our real friends are. Proverbs 17:17 says, "a friend loves at all times." Be there if possible when a friend needs you. Send them flowers before they die, not afterwards. Visit them in the hospital or nursing home, instead of the funeral home. Be there.

Recapping

- Find a great church and start going.
- Join a community service club.
- Go on a volunteer vacation or mission trip.
- Give 12 hugs a day.
- Accept others for who they are.
- Send five cards a week.
- Call three friends a week.
- Invite company for dinner once a month.
- Be quick to forgive.
- Be available.
- Look people in the eye and smile when greeting them.
- Be a host wherever you go.
- Be likable.

- Listen.
- Be a blessing and become a part of someone else's miracle.

"You have not lived a perfect day, unless you have done something for someone who will never be able to repay you."

Ruth Smeltzer

finances—Total Prosperity without a Ton of Money

You can be financially successful without being balanced, but you can't be balanced without being successful with your finances.

THE JOY OF MONEY

It's interesting to note that the pursuit of financial success causes people so much stress and for many of us, eventual burnout. Yet it is this very thing that is one of the five essential elements of real balance. This is referred to by many as "the paradox of success." To help understand the reason why, it may be helpful to look at some facts. Here are a few facts that may frighten you about North American people as they reach the age of 65:

- 45% are dependent on relatives (I'd better find some with money!).
- 30% are dependent on charity (I know, I've been supporting them!).
- 23% are still working (not a bad thing, if they want to be!).
- 2% are financially independent (meaning they can do what they want, when they want, with whom they choose).

Eighty percent of all North Americans owe more than they own. That's why this is such a great country; we can not only live above our means, but we can borrow to do so! Twenty percent of our income is used for consumer debt repayment. Wherever we are financially at the present time, it is a reflection of what we believe about ourselves. It is also a reflection of the level of our faith. Now, before you yell at me, read the next chapter on faith and see what I mean. I believe you'll agree with me, a poor self-image is the main barrier to financial success. In other words, both poverty and riches are the offspring of a person's thinking. The crop we reap is the same as the seeds we planted, just a whole lot more of it!

Our earlier conditioning and our environment determine our current attitude toward money and ourselves, which in turn has a dramatic effect on our ability to achieve financial success. People who think of themselves as poor will be poor. People who consider themselves failures will fail. When you think of yourself as blessed, you will be a blessing! When you think of yourself as wealthy, you will achieve wealth! When you think about yourself as a success, you will succeed!

"People who think lack, act lack!"

Bob Harrison

sweet success

There's much more to financial success than the amount you earn and how much of it you keep. The financial success I refer to as a vital ingredient of Real Balance is financial fitness, a condition of financial health. It's a state of financial freedom. Not Freedom 55, that suggests that if you hoard every penny between age 30 and 55 your net worth will be such that you will be able to retire without any worries. The question is, "how many years will you live, after you retire?" The statistics aren't very attractive. Why retire anyway? The word "retire" means to "withdraw from action or one's occupation." It is not the retreat from action or our occupations that kills so quickly after we retire, it's the imbalance that most people allow to take place. Inactivity stagnates and kills. We were created to make this world a better place, not just take up space. As we age, our center of balance shifts, but it still exists. Finances make up part of the balance equation because they meet a number of human needs we have each been created with.

Firstly, of course, our need for guarantee can be met by having what is normally referred to as financial security. But what's security anyway? A job? Ask someone who lost theirs recently due to downsizing, rightsizing, whatever. Is it a portfolio of stocks and mutual funds? Ask someone who invested in the gold exploration company Bre-X. Those investors got the shaft instead of the mine.

Having money in itself can lead us to believe we have security. Therefore, it does provide us with security as long as we have it. But many people need more than a guarantee when it comes to their money. Having all you need and keeping it safe can be a boring way to live. Most of us, when on our deathbeds, agree that risk is something we wish we had taken more of in our lives. Assess your need for gamble and match your need with the level of risk you take investing your money.

HOW MUCH IS ENOUGH?

When it comes to money, how much do we need to have before we feel as if we have enough? When can we say we're wealthy? Many times when I'm speaking to the media, doing an interview on a talk show or talking with a journalist who is writing an article, I'm asked what my definition of success is. When I was asked that question a year ago by a reporter for a local daily newspaper during an interview for an article they ran about me entitled "Back from Burnout," here's what I said: *"I have seen people earning $25,000 a year who are financially successful. And I have seen people earning $250,000 who are not financially successful....I don't measure financial success in terms of income. I don't measure it in terms of net worth. I say it's more of a feeling. A feeling of abundance, a feeling that God has blessed us with enough....Once you are to that point, you are free to bless others. It puts a whole new spin on things."*

Financial management can create the greatest stress. As someone who created enormous wealth early in life, and also suffered significant losses along the way, I can speak from experience on how to handle and survive success, financial and otherwise.

As in all areas of life, to be truly a success in the arena of our finances, we need to find a balance. A balance between getting it, keeping it, giving it away, investing it, protecting it and having fun with it. As we move through life, our center of balance shifts, but there's always a balance required. With each season of life there comes a shift in our priorities in the arena of our finances. As a child we are only concerned about spending our allowance; we don't care how our parents fund it. Then, as we realize our wants are greater than our piggy bank, we get our first job delivering papers or whatever. As we go through our school years we put a tremendous cash drain on our parents. However, this is a season; parents tend to kill themselves trying to buy all the designer clothes for their kids but fail to give them what the children need the most. Themselves.

A very popular book at present is *The Millionaire Next Door*. I received a copy from my financial adviser as a gift. What a book! In it you will find listed all the things self-made millionaires are willing to sacrifice to acquire a net worth of one million dollars. The list includes everything from their families to their faith. It extols the virtues of accumulating and hoarding vast amounts of money and does a great job of that. However, there's more to life than frugality and a ton of money in the bank.

Most people believe that if they earned more money they would be happy. They think that somehow, with a bigger income, their problems would disappear. However, the true joy doesn't come just from making the money, but also from sharing it with others. The power of money is truly amazing. If placed in the right hands it can help, heal and create value for you and others.

Getting It

The first key to mastering your financial life is the ability to create wealth. Notice, I didn't say earn wealth. True wealth cannot be earned, it must be created. We are all rewarded in direct proportion to our contribution to society. If we increase the value of what we contribute, our income will increase accordingly. The reason we look at creating wealth first is that unless we begin to create wealth, we have none to save, spend or share.

Here are some simple ways to begin to increase the value of what it is you contribute to society.

1. Start by asking yourself, "How can I achieve what I'm doing in less time? What would make me more valuable to my present employer, or could I perhaps run a home-based business besides my job?" Or, if you are already in business for yourself, it may mean you that you could increase output without increasing overhead. Increase volume without investing in more equipment. Spend a few days a week working from home and save on commuting time. Get yourself organized. We discuss this topic later on in the chapter on time management.

2. In what ways can you reduce production costs? Perhaps hire subcontractors who work out of their own home and you don't need to provide office space, telephone or free coffee. This is becoming a trend. There is such a thing now as a virtual assistant. With the technology available today, anything is possible. Become a customer instead of an employer by helping your employees start their own businesses and then subcontracting work to them. What a difference in attitude! They'll start bringing you gifts at Christmas time.

3. What career change would increase the value of my time? There may be some skill you have that, if it were developed, would increase the value of your time. The amount you are paid for each hour you work is a direct indicator of demand and supply for the skills you bring to the marketplace. Notice I didn't say the skills you have. It doesn't help much for you to have them,

if you don't bring them to the marketplace.

4. In marketing your product or service, you have two choices: You can compete or you can create. So many people and businesses only focus on how they can, or in many cases cannot, compete with the competition instead of spending time on daily basis to think, to be creative. Leaders create, followers compete. Be a creator!

5. Start to get money working for you, rather than you working for it. Again, it sounds too simple perhaps, but there are only two choices. Either you work for money or you have it work for you. An easy way to get money working for you is to purchase rental income property or invest in mutual funds or the stock market.

As you can see, earning more doesn't necessarily mean working longer hours. In many cases, if you'd simply cut back on the number of hours you are currently putting in at the office, you'd be more creative, more energetic, more dynamic, and the bottom line is—you'd be more valuable to your company or employer. You'd also have more time to look for real estate investments.

KEEPiNG It

Well, we've talked about earning or making money, now let's take a look at hanging on to it. Firstly, start paying less in income taxes. Most people I meet pay twice as much in income tax as they should. Start a home-based business. Split your income with your wife by contracting her services. Split your income with your children by setting up a family trust. Invest in a self-directed RRSP. To lower your tax rate, if you have young children, you should also consider investing in an RESP (Registered Educational Savings Plan) every month.

We've all heard it before, but I'll say it again anyway: *Pay yourself first.* That means before you pay your taxes. I can't believe how many people tell me how they'd like to start giving and investing to cut their taxes, but only see 50 to 70 percent of their paycheck. The rest is taken off before they even see it. That means someone else is getting paid first. Here's what you do to increase the "take home" amount of your next paycheck instead of letting the government have it interest-free for a year: Get yourself an application for Reduction of Tax at Source (RTS) at your local tax office and fill in the following information:

1. Alimony or Maintenance Payments (I guess this is our government's idea of an incentive to keep young families together). Attach a copy of your judgment or written separation agreement to your RTS.

2. RRSP Contributions—Simply sign a contract with your financial advisor to start investing in a self-directed RRSP (if you don't have a financial adviser, get one! I don't care if you're earning $30,000 a year, combined income). Invest 10 percent of your gross pay from every paycheck in an RRSP. Have the money deducted at source, and if you own your own business make sure you creditor proof it by investing it with a life insurance company. If your financial planner doesn't know about this stuff (some just don't bother because they are paid on commission), find another. Now attach a copy of that contract to your RTS.

3. Childcare Expenses—Unless you are a single parent, once you discover the benefits of staying at home, you won't need this one. If you are a single parent, start a daycare business from your home for other families where both spouses still work. Then, if you still have energy and love to meet people, get involved in a network marketing company in the evening once the kids are off to bed. You'll meet some of the finest, most positive, energetic, enthusiastic people at the rallies and training sessions these companies hold. I know, I've spoken to these people. They are so inspiring to speak to, I feel guilty taking my fee.

4. Interest and Carrying Expenses on Investment Loans—Any money you borrow to invest in real estate or mutual funds, even your house mortgage, can be used to reduce the amount of taxes you pay. Yes, even your house mortgage, if you borrowed against the equity in your home to finance your new business or finance any venture in the anticipation of making a profit. I

guess according to our tax department there are people who invest for reasons other than making a profit, such as simply to reduce taxes.

5. Charitable Donations—Every harvest contains a seed. Experience the miracle of giving 10 percent of your income to charity. This is the seed for your next harvest, as we'll discuss later on. For right now just take my word for it—it works! This one's a little tricky, but here's how you get the seed before the government does. You'll do a much better job of planting it anyway.

   Have a deduction made by your payroll department at source and direct it to the charity of choice. If your church or charity is on their approved list, make out postdated cheques and a letter from the treasurer and attach a copy to your RTS.

6. Rental and Self-Employed Losses—If you are running a home-based business besides your job, any losses can reduce your taxable income. Attach copies of year-end financial statements to your RTS. If your rental properties are showing a loss, attach a copy of your financial statements to your RTS. As you see, before you know it, you'll have the government sending you money, instead of vice versa.

7. Consider how you may actually save money by having a partner stay home instead of going out to work. Save the childcare expenses, extra clothing expenses, the extra car expenses, and split one partner's income by helping them do their job. There are so many ways to do this that have the approval of the tax department I could write an entire book on the subject. They may not love me for it, but I'm sure you would.

I've seen people reduce the amount of their weekly or biweekly deductions by 40 percent by just filling out this form and taking it to their employer. For one family, that meant a $12,000 increase per year in take-home pay. An extra $1,000 every month, which meant they could increase their giving from 5 to 10 percent, their RRSP investments from $50 a month to $300 a month, and they still had more left to spend than before. How is that possible? Well, the fact that 75 percent of the husband's earnings were now ending in the family's hands, instead of 55 percent, meant they now had more cash to give, to live on and to invest. As a result of these deductions, they now pay 20 percent less in taxes every year. All because they had an extra $1,000 each month to work with. Knowledge can be valuable.

The second key to hanging on to your wealth, needless to say, is spending less than you earn. As the saying goes, "If your outgo exceeds your income, your upkeep becomes your downfall." Sounds simple, but it's amazing how fast your spending catches up to your earning and quickly outpaces it if left unchecked. An excellent book packed with ideas on how to pay the lowest price for everything, is *Cut Your Spending In Half Without Settling for Less.*[17] Once you've found the best deal, pay for it with a credit card that gives you air miles. My favorite is CIBC's Aerogold Card that gives you one air mile for every dollar you spend. I pay for everything from utility bills to office supplies. My record is 40,390 miles in one month. That translates into 3 percent savings on all my purchases.

Pay down debt. Interest charges add up quickly, so pay down debt as fast as you can. First, pay off your high-interest consumer debt. That's the debt for which you can't write off the interest, debt you incurred to purchase items of a personal nature that will depreciate over time. Like your car. Secondly, by paying off your mortgage just a few years ahead of schedule, you can save tens of thousands of dollars. Banks tell you to make payments weekly, but the real savings are in shortening the amortization period. They don't tell you that, because they'd rather have you as a customer for 25 years than for 15 years.

Making It Grow

Multiplication of wealth comes from investing your money and the magic of compound interest. Compound interest means that your interest starts to earn you more interest. Even more exciting is the principle of **compound growth**. This is the way real estate properties increase in value over time. Think about what your parents paid for their house 25 years ago. The price they paid would seem ridiculously low in today's dollars. However, back then if you had told them what it would be worth today they probably would have laughed at you.

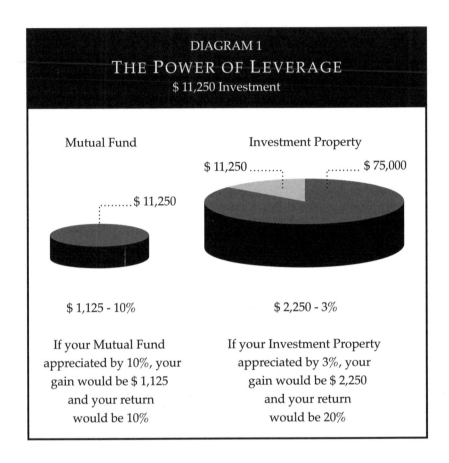

DIAGRAM 1
THE POWER OF LEVERAGE
$ 11,250 Investment

Mutual Fund   Investment Property

$ 11,250 .... $ 75,000

.........$ 11,250

$ 1,125 - 10% $ 2,250 - 3%

If your Mutual Fund   If your Investment Property
appreciated by 10%, your   appreciated by 3%, your
gain would be $ 1,125   gain would be $ 2,250
and your return   and your return
would be 10%   would be 20%

Leverage is the ability to purchase an asset with a small down payment. Take a look at Diagram 1, and see for yourself how a leveraged investment in real estate outperforms the same amount invested in a mutual fund. There's no comparison. What blows me away are the real estate agents out there with only mutual funds and no real estate in their investment portfolios. Wait till they see this! This is so easy anyone can do it, starting now. Yet it is so-o-o POWERFUL! This method of growing your wealth is called leverage. A lot riskier, but a whole lot more fun!

A good example of leverage is to purchase a piece of real estate for $100,000 with a 10 percent down payment. Suppose you sold that property in a year for $10,000 profit. That would be a 10 percent profit but it would be a 100 percent return on investment. However, in many cases, this can be done with little or no money down. It is simple to do.

Find a vendor that needs to sell. For instance, there are so many divorces happening and these people need to sell their homes in most cases. Here is a deal I found last week. This one is a "no-brainer." Here's how the deal could be done with very little of your own money:

Property:	9-year-old, 3-bedroom townhome located in Kitchener, Ontario
Situation:	Marriage split-up must sell, will rent back for 6 months
Paid:	$94,000
Asking:	$74,000
Mortgage:	$69,000 @ 6%
Facts:	Agent says owners will accept $72,000 even though that means husband and wife each need to kick in $500 to pay legals and commissions. Mortgage company will transfer mortgage to new purchaser.
Proposal:	Offer $69,000 and pay the real estate fees for the vendor. You can rent the property for $900 a month and get first and last month's rent up front. Use that $1,800 to pay the land transfer taxes. Since the vendors are willing to kick in $1,000, get them to pay your legal fees as well as theirs. However, you still need the money to pay the real estate commissions. If you always deal with the listing agent, they double-end the deal, meaning they get the listing and selling commission. You can usually get them to agree to accept 3 percent (or $2,200 in this case) with taxes. Here's how you get the money to pay the agent. The mortgage company will let you miss up to three consecutive payments if your cash flow so dictates. Since the first payment isn't due

anyway until the end of the first month, give the second and third rent checks to the agent instead of paying the mortgage. It's not that difficult.

This property is now yours with no money down and yielding $100 a month positive cash flow. In 25 years the property is yours free and clear, worth at least twice the price you bought it for, and your tenants have paid for it! This what you call leverage. It's amazing! It's powerful! It's fun! What a way to build an investment portfolio that will not only generate an income in your golden years, but also give you something to keep you occupied. While you're at it and you're feeling generous, since this usually doesn't take any of your money anyway, buy one for each of your kids to teach them the art of creative financing and the power of leverage.

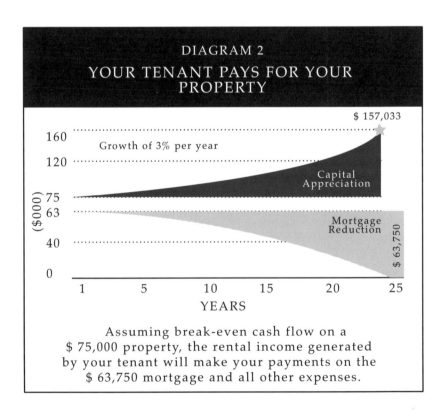

DIAGRAM 2
YOUR TENANT PAYS FOR YOUR PROPERTY

$ 157,033

Growth of 3% per year

Capital Appreciation

Mortgage Reduction

$ 63,750

($000)

YEARS

Assuming break-even cash flow on a $ 75,000 property, the rental income generated by your tenant will make your payments on the $ 63,750 mortgage and all other expenses.

Keeping It Safe

When was the last time you reviewed your insurance coverage? Do you have adequate life insurance, automobile insurance and home insurance, and are you getting the best deal possible? Insurance is something you buy with the hope you'll never need it, especially life or disability insurance. My wife's uncle Eli was as healthy as a horse. He was never sick that I could remember. He never exercised more strenuously than a round of golf and he didn't worry at all about his diet. He was so healthy that a year ago he cancelled his life insurance policy, thinking he didn't need it. He was right, he wouldn't need it. But his wife would! Six months later, one Saturday morning, he got out of bed, took one step, and keeled over. Dead of a heart attack at 65. Life insurance is for those we love and leave behind. Be responsible and make certain you have adequate coverage.

However, when it comes to asset protection, there's more than insurance to look at. In today's society, where most people seem anxious to sue the next person, asset protection is a very important subject. The wealthy have their heads above the crowd and are the ones susceptible to lawsuits, many of which are frivolous. It's one thing to have your home insured against fire, theft and burglary. It's another thing to protect it from your creditors. The best advice here is to consult an expert *before* you need to. These experts are expensive and hard to find but their advice can be worth many times what you pay for it. Here are a few tips I've learned from them:

- If you are the main income earner, ownership of your major assets such as your home and real estate investments should be held in your spouse's name. This move protects your family home from creditors while your secured creditors may otherwise liquidate it at a fire-sale price.
- Be certain to place your retirement savings with a life insurance company to keep them creditor proof. Creditor proofing is not a way around paying your creditors in the event of financial disaster. Rather, it's a way of staying in control of life while going through the experience, allowing you to rebound much quicker

without having to declare bankruptcy. The quicker you get back on top, the sooner you can work at repaying your creditors.

- Pay your life insurance premium personally with after-tax dollars if you are self-employed, so that in the event of your death, the proceeds will be tax-free to your heirs. Get the cheapest insurance you can get with the goal of being self-insured by the time you are 60. Only get as much insurance coverage as you need and reduce the coverage as your need for coverage changes. At one time I had five million dollars' worth of coverage. I would joke with my wife that I was worth more to her dead than alive!

- Keep your will up to date. If you die intestate (without a will), your assets will be distributed according to government regulations. Consider having your children receive yearly payments until they reach the age of 25 instead of lump sum payments. The average length of time it takes to spend a lottery windfall is six months, no matter how large or small the amount. The same goes for inheritances.

- Make certain you have completed a living trust. This document sets out who will act as your trustee in the event you are incapacitated. This person could be your spouse or a personal friend. If no one is named, your spouse may be forced to stand back while the government steps in to manage your affairs. Perish the thought!

- Get appraisals on your jewelry. This is a lesson we learned the hard way after we were robbed five years ago and discovered only $6,000 of the $16,000 worth of jewelry that was stolen was covered, because we didn't have appraisals.

There are, however, two assets that I have found to be not only valuable, but also totally creditor proof: what you gain by experience and what you give away with no strings attached. So you see, there is no way you can lose everything.

What's the point to earning, maintaining and protecting your wealth if you are not going to enjoy it? When it comes to money, the hardest part to learn, for some, is to simply enjoy spending it.

Havin' Fun With It

Too many people wait for retirement to spend or enjoy their wealth. Unfortunately, many never make it to that stage of life. They die before they get a chance to enjoy it! I love the bumper sticker I saw on the back of a motorhome; it read, "We're spending our kids' inheritance." Too often we die before we take the opportunity to live. How tragic. Reminds me of the story about the little boy who walks up to Grandpa and says, "Grandpa, can you make a sound like a frog?" "Why would you ask that question, Johnny?" Grandpa asked. Johnny replied, "Cuz last night I was talking to Grandma, and she said when you croak we're all going to Hawaii."

Start right now to enjoy your wealth by rewarding yourself on occasion for a job well done. Begin now to celebrate your victories. End your existence and begin to live. It's a lot more fun. However, there's no joy like the joy of giving it away. It plants the seed for future harvest and at the same time meets our need to give.

Now before I finish talking about sharing our wealth let me say this: Nothing gives more enjoyment than sharing your wealth. So you see, you can't really enjoy your wealth unless you give it away.

> **"Misers aren't much fun to live with, but they make wonderful ancestors."**
>
> Terry Gillespey

Giving It Away

The law of giving, like the law of the harvest, is another universal success principle that operates whether we believe in it or not. This law of giving is found in the Bible. Luke 6:38 says, "If you give, you will receive. Your gift will return to you in full measure, pressed down, shaken together to make room for more, and running over. Whatever measure you use in giving—large or small—it will be used to measure what is given back to you."

Give Your Best

If you want the best, give the best. Too many people only give away their garbage and wonder why that's all they get out of life.

The favorite excuse for people not to give is that they "can't afford to" or they are "short of cash." Let me tell you from experience, you can't afford not to. Let's be honest; we can afford anything within reason if it's a priority and we want it badly enough. Unless giving becomes a priority, there will never be enough time or money left to give. Give your best, not your leftovers.

So often I hear people say, "I'll start giving after all my debts are paid off." That's like saying, "I'll start to plant after I harvest my first crop." The law of giving only works one way: "Give and it shall be given unto you." The law of the harvest is exactly the same: we reap what we sow, not vice versa. Nowhere will you ever find these laws operating in reverse. We must always give or plant first. We must also always plant or give whatever it is we expect to harvest or receive in return.

Give Wisely

I believe your tithe, or 10 percent of your income, belongs to the ministry that feeds you spiritually. The balance of your giving should go to worthwhile charitable organizations that are financially responsible and accountable, or wherever you see a need. Learn to listen to your heart. It will tell you what to do.

Give With Joy

Giving must be joyfully done for it to be effective. Nothing in the world is more satisfying or more fun than giving, if your attitude is right. I hate to receive a gift if I know the giver is reluctant to give it. We all love a cheerful giver, and so does God.

Plan your giving by placing into your personal budget, at the beginning of each year, an item called charitable donations. Budget your giving right after your income and just before your taxes. Last-minute "panic giving" can often take place with a grudging attitude. Plan your giving and become a joyful giver.

Abundant living requires abundant giving.

Finally, let's talk about risk—without it you can never experience true financial freedom. Most people won't step out of the boat, yet they expect to walk on the water. Most people tiptoe through life, playing it safe, hoping to arrive safely at retirement, and arrive only to find they now regret the fact that they never dared to venture outside their comfort zone. They feel they have wasted so much of their potential. Then again, they will never really know what their potential was, because they never dared to win. They never stepped out in faith because of the fear they might sink. Instead, they sat in the boat until it sank. That is existing, not living!

We either step forward into fear or back into safety. We were born to win, but conditioned to lose. We let other people put a lid on our potential. Get out of the boat, step onto the water and watch the miracles happen in your life. Go for it! All things are possible for those who believe. So instead of saying you'll believe it when you see it, start believing. You will see it.

Risks must be taken, because the greatest hazard in life is to risk nothing. The person who risks nothing does nothing, has nothing and is nothing. There is no success or failure without risk!

You may avoid suffering and sorrow, but simply cannot learn, feel, change, grow, love and live, without risk. Chained by the certitudes, you are a slave who has forfeited freedom. You are only free if you take risks!

Now let's look at three simple steps to get us started down the road to financial freedom and real balance:

First, find out where you are in the following areas:
- attitude with regard to money
- cash flow (money coming in and going out)
- assets, liabilities and net worth
- debts and minimum monthly payments
- life, auto and property insurance
- will/power of attorney

Second, decide where you'd like to be:
- cash flow (create a spending plan)
- net worth
- things
- giving
- insurance

Third, set goals and develop an action plan. We discover how in the chapter on goal setting.

Recapping

- Write out your own definition of "success."
- Believe you have unlimited potential for financial growth and success.
- Take personal responsibility for your financial achievements.
- Create a written spending plan (lots more fun than a budget!).
- Pay yourself first. You deserve it. You earned it!
- Explore ways to reduce your tax bill. Take the time to strategize!
- Learn how to pay the lowest price for everything. You'll have more to give and enjoy!
- Contribute to your RRSP but live to the limit today. It's all we have!
- Consider an RESP. It's a way of saying to your children, "I believe you're going to the top!"
- Buy investment real estate. With the average price of Canadian real estate increasing between 8 and 9 percent over the past 25 years, it's a safe bet. And your tenants help build your net worth. Excellent retirement plan!
- Pay down consumer debt. This is debt on which you can't write off the interest.
- Review your insurance needs. Get only as much as you need, paying as little as possible, but make sure you have enough!
- Have an estate plan and will. Estate planning is easier while you're alive!

- Give with joy. Give while you are alive! People who plan to give, give four times more than those who don't!
- Simplify your life.

"Money is the root of all evil, but the stem of happiness."

Theresa Kubassek (Mom)

Faith—Believing in More than Yourself

All things are possible to them who believe. However,
all things are probable to them who have faith.

Rich in Faith

We've been dealing with the concept of balance in discussing the five
"F" words, so it would be difficult to say any one area is more important than any other. But faith has played an enormous role in my life,
not just faith in myself, but also faith in others and faith in my
Creator—belief in something greater than myself. With my unique
upbringing on the Community Farm of the Brethren, I searched to
define my faith, and integrate life principles instilled through my religious training.

I'm the first to admit that as I achieved success in various businesses, and got preoccupied running them, I had less time for people, and
stopped communicating with my Creator. I learned my lessons. I
reconnected with what was important in my life. I re-established a
connection with the God who created me. A connection to a power
source far greater than I am. A relationship rather than a religion.
Faith in an all-powerful, all-knowing Creator. Dr Flach in his book
Resilience states, "I believe the most vital ingredient of resilience is
faith."[18]

Seeing Without Seeing

What is faith? The Bible says faith is the substance of things hoped for and the evidence of things not seen. It is the confident assurance that what we are believing, is going to happen. Faith is not knowing what is possible, but rather believing the impossible even though we don't see it. George MacDonald once quipped, "Seeing isn't believing. It's only seeing." Faith is seeing without seeing. Faith is exciting! Faith is the end of anxiety. It combines assurance and anticipation. The assurance that all will work out for the best, and the anticipation of seeing how! Faith is belief that has matured to the point where we take action.

Belief is believing that an egg yolk will turn into a chicken. Faith is putting that egg into an incubator and trusting it will hatch. Belief is believing every seed contains a harvest. Faith is planting the seed, maintaining it and preparing for the harvest. Action is the key difference between belief and faith. A few thousand years ago this guy by the name of Noah believed there was a God. He also had faith. He had enough faith to build a ship in the middle of dry land. He was warned about something he couldn't see, and took action anyway. That was an act of faith. The result? His family was saved.

Beliefs control our thoughts, but faith is what gets us into the action. Beliefs help us draw the map, but faith inspires us to start the journey. Belief makes things possible, faith makes things probable. Faith without works is not faith. Faith without action is only theory. Without action, it's dead! Real faith takes action. It propels us in the direction of our purpose and our goals at lightning speed. But before you can have faith, you must believe. Before we can have faith in ourselves, we must believe. Believe we have limitless potential, believe that the power within us is greater than the power in the world around us. Believe that we are supernatural beings created in the likeness of our Creator. Before we can have faith in God, we must believe He exists.

I'm sure you must be thinking, *don't get religious on me now*. Relax, I won't. I am sure, though, you would love to know how to get faith without getting religion. No, that's not an oxymoron. It is possible to have faith without being religious. Here is how. Faith comes by hearing, the same as doubt comes by hearing. However, doubt comes from listening to your family and your friends who believe it is their

God-given calling to rain on your parade because they don't have one of their own. They are the ones who chuckle when you tell them you believe you can write a book. "On what?" they laugh. Now you begin to doubt. They planted the seeds of doubt. It's our choice whether or not to let them take root. If you do, you reap a harvest of mediocrity and apathy. Then your friends will feel better. You are back to their level of thinking. On the other hand, faith comes the same way.

"Faith comes by hearing the word,"[19] says the Bible. If faith in God comes by hearing His word, faith in others and ourselves must come the same way. By hearing the word. Hearing can only happen if we listen. To listen we must stop talking. However, sometimes it is up to us speak the word, so that others and we ourselves can hear it. If a child hears once that he or she has potential, he or she may believe. But if that child hears that same encouragement over and over, that child will begin to have faith in their abilities. The same goes when we encourage other people we interact with on a regular basis. The same rule applies to hearing about God on a regular basis. We begin by believing in Him and then move to the next level of having faith in Him. We begin with a little faith and, as we exercise it, it grows.

Without belief there can be no faith, without faith there can be no vision.

Faith in Yourself

Faith in one's self is generally referred to as self-esteem. It is our belief in the skills, abilities and talents we possess that empowers us to have faith in ourselves. It is our environment since early childhood that has shaped our beliefs. It is, therefore, environment that determines the level of faith we as humans have in ourselves. The first step to increase in the area of self-esteem is to change our environment. However, in order to change something we need to know what it is.

Our environment consists of the objects and conditions that surround us. It's our family, and our friends. It's the words we hear, and the words we speak. It's the church we attend, and the office or factory we work in. It's the car we drive, and the home we live in. It's the magnets we have on the fridge door, and the sayings we have on our T-shirts. It's the books we read, and the tapes we listen to. It's the spouse we are married to, and the in-laws who came along. It is the beauty of nature around us, and the bustle of traffic. It's the energy you feel sometimes when you enter a room, and it's the peace and quiet of solitude. You can't change the environment you lived in yesterday, but you can decide to change the environment you live in today. Believe in yourself. You can do it! Within you is the power to do things you've never even dreamed of. This becomes available as soon as you change your beliefs.

"The future belongs to those who believe in the beauty of their dreams."

Eleanor Roosevelt

Motivating people is telling them they can do it. Getting them to believe in themselves. Making them believe the limits they have are the ones they put on themselves. But that's not enough. The next step is inspiration. Inspiring people is helping them become the kind of person who acts like the person they would like to be. It's about becoming, not just achieving. Motivation instills belief; inspiration instills faith. Goal setting requires us to believe in ourselves. Goal getting requires faith. Belief enables us; faith empowers us.

All children are born to win. Unfortunately many are programmed to fail. If you grew up in a home without love and structure, your self-image may be one of the obstacles you need to overcome. Our earlier conditioning determines our current attitude. Attitude is our outward expression of an inward feeling. This is a key point, since our feelings are a result of our actions in the first place. To break the bad attitude cycle, you must begin to act right whether you feel like it or not.

"What lies behind us and what lies before us are tiny matters compared to what lies within us."

Ralph Waldo Emerson

Faith in Others

Late one afternoon a little girl was playing in her backyard and climbed up an old maple tree. She climbed about halfway to the top. Realizing how far up she had climbed she became frightened. It was starting to get dark outside, making it difficult to see. So she began climbing back down and soon found herself stuck in the middle of the tree. The sun had finally set and the little girl was becoming even more frightened. She started to cry, and began yelling as loud as she could to get the attention of her parents.

Her father heard her from inside the house, ran out to the backyard and said, "What's wrong, Sharon? Are you all right? Where are you? I can't see you." The little girl cried out, "Daddy, I'm stuck up here in the tree and I can't get down. I'm scared." The father said, "Don't worry, I'll get you down." The father walked up to the tree and saw her standing on a branch only a few feet above the ground. The tree was heavily covered with leaves and branches blocking the little girl's vision. The father looked up at his daughter and said, "Jump. Don't be afraid, I'll catch you." The little girl hesitated, "I can't jump, it's too dark, and I can't see you." The father answered, "That's all right, honey, I can see you."

Faith is believing in a person, idea or thing when common sense tells us not to. We all have within us the need to share and give into someone else's life. We have the need for significance—to know we are loved. By giving and sharing love with others, we receive love ourselves. It's the law of the harvest, remember? We also have within each of us human beings the need to be part of a group, to have fellowship. I believe this is where a church can meet an important need we each have. In my study of highly successful people, those who stay healthy when they reach the top have a strong religious involvement. The church is a vital part of their lives. The shaping of their character began with the training they received as a child—training in attitude, work ethic and moral standards.

Our need for fellowship can be met by belonging to a service club or professional association as well. However, since every one of us has a need for growth in our lives, and part of that growth is spiritual, attending church can meet the need for fellowship and growth at the same time. Fellowship is the only thing we can't do alone.

When things are going well, most of us think we are a tower unto ourselves. We don't need others to help us achieve our goals. We can do this ourselves. However, when the going gets rough, it's incredibly reassuring to know that there are others we can lean on. This faith comes by first believing, believing that basically all people are honest, trustworthy and want you to succeed. Now, I know that's not always true, but if you are ever going to believe in others, you need to give them the benefit of the doubt.

Love

"But the greatest of these is love."[20] Dr Selye in his book *Stress Without Distress* says, "The effort to 'love thy neighbor as thyself' probably has done more good, and more to make life pleasant, than any other guideline."[21] Once we have accepted the love of God and have allowed it to fill us, it becomes a powerful weapon. As this love spills out of us, it heals our relationships with the people around us. It creates community and restores our belief in our fellow humans. This love for one another is the indicator that we believe. Without belief, there can be no love.

Believing in others is just that. Believing. Faith in others is when you believe enough to actually take action. You not only believe they will give help, you ask them for it. You not only believe they can help you succeed in your business, but you ask them to share their leads. You not only believe they would pray for you if you asked them, you ask them to when you need it. When we love enough to take action, our belief has become faith.

Rejoice in the success of others as if it were your own. They will begin to believe you really care about them. When they believe you really care, that's when they will begin to trust you. It is that trust that is an indicator of the faith we have in others.

Faith in God

> "Unbelief puts our circumstances between God and us. Faith puts God between our circumstances and us."
>
> F.B. Meyer

If you have been feeling overwhelmed and out of control, take your eyes off your circumstances and put more faith in God. Faith in God is based on evidence but not scientific data. His handiwork in creation, the miracles Christ performed while He was here on earth, and the change He brings about in the hearts of men and women are all evidence that God does exist and that he intervenes in the lives of people. Here are some of the characteristics of a true faith in God:

Faith in God believes the incredible. Many say, "I cannot believe the story of creation. I just can't believe that miracles happen, that there is a heaven, that there is such a thing as eternity." Hebrews 11:3 says, "By faith we understand that the universe was created at God's command."

Faith in God hears the inaudible. There are about 9000 radio signals in a metropolitan area, but without the aid of radio equipment, the words and music go undetected by people. Likewise, faith is the faculty that enables us to sense God's direction and reassurance.

Faith in God sees the invisible. When the Russian cosmonaut Gherman Titov returned from space, he said, "I looked for God but I didn't see him." However, when American astronaut James McDivitt returned, his statement was vastly different: "I did not see God looking into my space cabin window...but I could recognize His work in stars...." One possessed the inner eye of faith and the other didn't.

Faith in God accomplishes the impossible. First faith thinks the unthinkable, and then proceeds to accomplish the impossible. Charles Haddon Spurgeon said God delights in impossibilities: "One man says, I will do as much as I can. Any fool can do that. He that believes in God does what he cannot do, attempts the impossible, and performs it." Jesus said, "If you have faith as a mustard seed…nothing shall be impossible to you."

Faith is an aptitude that can increase in strength and improve in quality when properly exercised. The greatest faith we can achieve is to believe when God's hand is still and His voice is silent. A victim of the Holocaust scratched these words into the crumbling wall of his home before his death: "I believe in the sun—even when it does not shine; I believe in love—even when it is not shown; I believe in God—even when He does not speak."

> **"If you believe, you will receive whatever you ask for in prayer."**
>
> Matthew 21:22

BUiLDiNG YOUR FaiTH

Every time we take a risk, there is stress created in our bodies. Perhaps it would be fair to say that the stress results from the anxiety of not knowing the outcome of the decisions we make. This is where our faith in God is helpful since He knows the end from the beginning. When we take our faith and place it entirely in ourselves, we are subjecting our bodies and minds to unnecessary stress.

Taking risks and trusting for the results is the way we build our faith. It's exercising our faith muscles that makes them stronger. It is pushing the envelope in our personal life that boosts our self-esteem. It is the achievement of our goals that builds faith in ourselves. The same works as we put trust in our friends in the time of need, and they come through for us; the next time we don't hesitate to call. We believe they'll be there to help. More than that, we have faith in them, so we call.

"Don't let the fear of striking out hold you back."
Babe Ruth (1895-1948)
(Ruth held the all-time record for home runs…
and strikeouts!)

As we put our trust in God and he comes through for us, we begin to build our faith in Him. When we get to the point that we realize "He never lets us down," there is a sense of peace that comes over us that nothing can destroy. Faith is the end of worry, doubt and anxiety. It is the beginning of peace, harmony and hope. It is living one day at a time instead of worrying about tomorrow or dwelling on the failures in our past. Faith is praying for today's bread, not tomorrow's.

Most people sleep half an hour too long every day. They jump out of bed, throw on some clothes, jump into the car and head for work, gulping down a cup of coffee while dodging traffic. By the time they reach the office they're ready for a tranquilizer. That kind of routine does not make for starting your day in a frame of mind that is happy, peaceful, positive and powerful.

Before my burnout experience, that was how I started every day. As I began recovering from burnout, I made a commitment to dedicate the first hour of every day to meditation, singing, prayer, goal setting, reading and physical exercise in solitude. This has since become a high priority in my life. I'm positive because I decided to

Son, don't bother to give God instructions — just report for duty.

be positive when I got out of bed this morning. I believe the stage is set for each day during the first hour. Here's how I go about setting the stage for my day.

The first thing I had to do was to form the habit of early rising. I had never been an early riser; my mom called me a night owl. But what better time of the day to get yourself in tune with the God who controls the universe than early in the morning, when all is quiet and your mind is alert and fresh?

THE POWER OF PRAYER

I begin my prayer time by giving thanks for all the good things in my life.

- A beautiful spouse, who loves and cares for me
- Four wonderful kids
- My mom, dad, brothers and sisters
- A creative mind and healthy body
- My Creator, who supplies all my needs
- An abundantly happy and successful life
- Prosperous businesses and projects in which I am involved
- My church and friends

Secondly, I forgive all the people in my life.

Then I confess to God my shortcomings and thank him for His forgiveness and the clean slate with which I can now begin my day.

Next, I turn my thoughts to my own personal needs, challenges and opportunities, believing that God wants the best for my life and that I'll receive what I ask for. I ask in detail.

I ask for divine wisdom to fill my being, so that I may be ready at all times to make wise, intelligent and timely decisions.

Wisdom is my number one prayer request, because I believe to have God's wisdom is to hold the keys to the abundant life He desires us to live. I then ask Him to meet any financial, physical or other needs that I may have.

Finally, my daily prayer is that I may be a blessing to everyone I meet and that my cup will be full and running over. I pray that I will prosper in all my ways, and that I will be blest, so that I can be a blessing to others. I then thank God again for all the wonderful things He means to me and for the personal relationship I can have with my Creator.

To conclude my power hour, I take a warm shower. While the warm water flows over my body, I sing and think happy, positive thoughts. I simply let the water wash away any negative thoughts or tiredness from my body.

Before I have breakfast, I spend 10 to 15 minutes with my wife, praying and reading the Bible together. The Book of Proverbs contains a vast amount of practical wisdom for operating a business and also contains many successful living principles. We conclude our time together with prayer, asking God's blessing on each other for the day, before we part. The support of those we love is so vital to our success as human beings that, without it, we would never reach full potential in any area of our lives.

Balancing Your Faith

Achieving life balance in the area of faith, as we have just discovered, requires a balance between our faith in God, faith in ourselves and faith in our fellow humans. We can't love God if we don't love ourselves. Without faith in ourselves how could we possibly believe in a Creator who created us in his own likeness? Faith is absolutely necessary to overcome fear. Faith and fear cannot live in the same mind.

Having faith in ourselves, faith in others and faith in God helps to bring fulfillment and balance in our lives. With faith in God, there's hope for the soul; with faith in others, we can enjoy the trust and joys of friendship; with faith in ourselves, it is possible to overcome life's obstacles and begin again. Faith says tomorrow can be brighter, no matter how cloudy yesterday was.

Recapping

- All things are possible to those who believe!
- Believe in yourself. Your potential is limitless!
- Believe in others. Their support will be valuable when you need it.
- Believe in God. He controls the universe.
- Have faith. With faith all things are probable!
- Keep building your faith. Exercise it regularly. Take risks.
- Keep your faith in balance—a balance of faith in yourself, faith in others and faith in your Creator.

PART THREE: BRINGING IT ALL TOGETHER

"It is possible to give freely and become more wealthy, but those who are stingy will lose everything. The generous prosper and are satisfied; those who refresh others will themselves be refreshed."

Proverbs 11:24-25

RiSinG FRΩM THe ASHeS

"There is no medicine like hope, no incentive so great and no tonic so powerful as the expectation of something better tomorrow."

O.S. Marden

HΩPe

"And now these three remain: faith, hope and love."[22] Hope is only possible if it is preceded by faith. Without faith, there can be no hope. "The Encyclopedia Britannica has columns on love and faith, but not a single word about hope," observed the late psychiatrist Dr. Karl Menninger.[23] Perhaps you are someone who picked up this book expecting to find that four-letter word, the one the media says I swear by—hope. Perhaps you've experienced failure recently, or not so recently. Life came along and dealt you a blow from which you have not yet recovered. Perhaps it was a financial failure, perhaps it was a failure with your family or perhaps it was with your health. You've been knocked down and have stayed down. You have lost hope. You feel like such a failure.

In *Succeed Without Burnout,* I shared how I went through all three failures at some point in time. One thing I learned was this: *Failure's not a person, it's only an event.* No matter what obstacle you face, it's possible to overcome it. All you need is hope. With hope we get back up and try again. I believe you will find that hope in this chapter and in this book.

Forgive and Forget

In order to overcome any of life's obstacles and rise from the ashes of our despair, it's important for us to understand a few basic rules. First, if the failure experience was your fault and you've had the guts to take responsibility for it, forgive yourself immediately. If it was someone else's fault, forgive them. Stop carrying the load of unforgivingness, it's too heavy! Second, stop linking your present failure to previous failures.

Every failure experience contains lessons. Not just for us, but for the rest of world as well, if we have the guts and humility to share them. No one will live long enough to make all the mistakes themselves, so it's our duty to share the lessons we learn. That's what this book is all about. Sharing lessons learned. Make sure you learn the lesson in your failure and then move on. Caution, though, lessons not learned will need to be repeated. The unfortunate thing is that following lesson-learning experiences, many times people can't stop beating themselves up, and as a result they refuse to take future risks.

No Fear

Without faith we retreat into fear. Fear can hold us captive. The key is to *find* faith. It can be found, even if perhaps you thought you had lost yours for good. Reading and listening to encouraging information is the place to start. Congratulations, you've already started. Feed your mind a diet of the most positive, truthful, hope-inspiring information you can find. It will set you free! It will set you free and you will start to take some shots on goal, knowing full well some will miss the net. You will discover it's not what happens to you that counts. It's what happens in you that really matters!

When our focus is only on what we are achieving, and not on who we are becoming in the process, failure can be devastating. Stop thinking about what's happened to you. Start thinking about what's happening in you. Are you a more compassionate person? I know I am! Are you more understanding and empathetic of others in the same situation? You can only say, "I know where you're coming from," if you've been there. What an attitude adjustment failure can be.

We decide if failure improves our attitude or makes it worse. Our attitude is our outward expression of our inward feelings. It is how we express, on the outside, what's going on inside. Smile even if you don't feel like it. Sing even if you'd rather pout. Before you know it, you'll feel like singing. Give your pity parties a time limit. With a can-do attitude we try, even when we don't feel like it! You may be only an attitude away from winning again.

Knowing the way is not going the way.

CRiPPleD BUt Not DiSaBleD

Physical injuries can get some people down and keep them down while others flap their wings and begin to soar higher. A perfect example is my friend and fellow pilot, Carl Hiebert, the author of *Gift of Wings* and *Us Little People*. As a result of a hang-gliding accident, Carl injured his back and has been a paraplegic ever since. Carl was still in rehab when he took up flying ultralight aircraft. He has since flown across Canada photographing our beautiful country and traveled the world as a motivational speaker. I have had him up in my helicopter a few times and he has asked me if I'll give him some lessons. He ignored my comment that you need both hands and both feet to fly a chopper. He just doesn't give up. What an inspiration!

Carl hosts a fly-in once a year and invites his friends to join him for a barbecue at the farm where he keeps his airplane. I joined him and his friends a couple of years ago, flying in with my helicopter. Carl raffled off a few tickets for free helicopter rides. The holder of one of the tickets drawn was an older gentleman in his mid-sixties. It's funny how "old" is always 25 years older than you are. However, this gentleman insisted that his wife get the free ride. I agreed, and he brought his wife over and introduced her to me. She appeared to be the same age but she was completely blind.

What an experience! As we took off, I quickly realized that I needed to be her eyes, so that she too could enjoy the beautiful scenery. I began to describe the sight below. The beautiful green trees, the crops in the fields and the winding Nith River. I described the beauty of Creation below us as well as my limited vocabulary would permit. This lady was just in awe as she kept saying, "WOW! This is so-o-o beautiful." I saw with amazement how grateful she was to experience the world through my eyes. (Close your eyes for a minute to understand the view she actually had.)

I felt a tear coming to my eyes as I realized that with the attitude this lady had, the rest of the world was blinder than she was. Think about it. Who's better off, the person who can't see or the person who won't? Who's better off, the person who doesn't have a dream, or the person who has one but won't follow it?

No Coincidence

Once you understand that nothing happens by accident or coincidence, you will realize there's a purpose for every event that happens in our lives. You are here for a purpose. Follow that purpose and you find the passion for your dreams you thought was gone forever. With passion your productivity will return.

If you are reading this, think how much more fortunate you are than my blind passenger. Take time to watch a sunset. Instead of complaining about what you don't have, begin to give thanks for things you've been taking for granted. Whatever we focus on gets bigger. Start to focus on your assets and blessings. When we begin to count our blessings, our problems have a way of shrinking.

With gratitude comes hope. With hope, we begin to set goals once again. You start planting again, with the faith that you will harvest.

Ben Kubassek

Don't give up. Don't ever, ever quit!

Here's a poem my daughter Krystal recently stuck to the wall above my desk:

Don't Quit

When things go wrong, as they sometimes will,
When the road you're trudging seems all uphill,
When the funds are low and the debts are high,
And you want to smile, but you have to sigh,
When care is pressing you down,
Rest if you must—but don't you quit.

Life is queer with its twists and turns,
As every one of us sometimes learns,
And many a person turns about
When they might have won if they'd stuck it out;
Don't give up, though the pace seems slow —
You may succeed with another blow.

Success is failure turned inside out —
The silver tint of the clouds of doubt —
And you never can tell how close you are,
It may be near when it seems afar;
So stick to the fight when you're hardest hit —
It's when things seem worst you mustn't quit!

Clinton Howell

Setting Balanced Goals

"Far better it is to dare mighty things, to win glorious triumphs even though checkered by failures, than to rank with those poor spirits who neither enjoy much nor suffer much because they live in the gray twilight that knows neither victory nor defeat."
Theodore Roosevelt (1858-1919)

Goals Versus Daydreams

Many people wish their lives were different. They wish they had more money. They wish they had a better car. They wish they owned a bigger home. If you've had similar wishes over the years, have you made any progress toward them? If you hear others stating their wishes, do you actually think for a second that they are going attain them? Not likely.

Wishes and daydreams aren't all bad. They can be the visualization of a future harvest. They may be the inspiration you need to plant the seed that will yield your harvest. These wishes and daydreams are the forerunners to a goal. Just as beliefs require action to become faith, wishes require action in order to become goals. Wishing involves only thought, but goal setting requires action to be added to that thought. A goal is a desired result, or outcome, for which you have developed an action plan for achievement.

My goal is to move you from wishing to goal setting. From goal setting to goal getting. To get started, the key is to eliminate the time between the thought and the action. This time is generally referred to as procrastination. Or if you're real religious, this is the time you spend praying. Nothing wrong with praying, prayer can move mountains, but sooner or later it's time to act. Too many people are waiting for just the right time.

Raising the Bar

The key with goal setting is keep your goals challenging enough to be exciting, but attainable enough to be reached. They should make you reach, but not for the stars. Goals that are unrealistic, and out of sight, can be frustrating and lead to burnout, as in my case. I never really allowed myself to achieve any of my goals. If it looked like I was going to clear a hurdle, I would quickly raise the bar higher.

Keep your goals in sight and in focus. Keep them positive in nature. Be prepared to support your goals with energy, enthusiasm and effort. Make that commitment now or skip ahead to the next chapter. Better still, give this book to someone who will make the commitment.

Make It Measurable

A goal must be measurable in order to be a goal. If it is not measurable, how can we tell if what we have achieved is the result or outcome we desired in the first place? We can't. Without some means of measurement it is also impossible to track our progress. Without the ability to track progress, it's very difficult to stay motivated or even know if we are still on the right track. It is just deciding to travel in your car to Toronto and your map says it is 100 miles to the east. You have a measurable goal. So you begin traveling, and an hour later you see a road sign that says "Toronto 50 miles." That is an encouragement because before you started you knew how far you had to travel, and you are now able to measure your progress.

It also helps to set short-term (6-month) goals, as well as mid-term (2-3 year) goals, and life goals (however long that may be!).

Going Public

Going public with your goals can be a scary thing to do. Scary, but at the same time helpful. Not necessarily helpful in setting your goal, but possibly very helpful in getting your goal. Sharing with 100 people my goal to write my first book was a key factor in actually completing it. Everyone kept asking me, "How's the book coming?" Share your goals with those who love and support you.

Under Review

Review your goals regularly. If they are on your computer, place a shortcut to them on your desktop. Or if you drive a lot, put a copy above your sun visor (to be reviewed only while waiting at stoplights, of course). I can hear the Triple A personalities like me saying, "Yeah, right!" The point is keep your goals handy for quick review, without having to dig them out of your *piling system*. Regular review helps remind us of the seeds we've planted, and encourages us to keep nurturing those seeds before they sprout and break through the ground.

Many times there is not an incremental progress toward the achievement of our goals. We set a goal to start eating right and exercising. Just as it took time to gain the weight and get out of shape, it takes a few weeks or months to see the fruits of the seeds we've planted. Learning a new skill or language is the much the same. Many times we get bored learning the basics or the rules of grammar because it seems as if so little progress is being made initially. As a result, we lose interest in our goals, we stop watering the seed we've planted and it fails to come to life. So we start the process all over with a new goal. That's the reason some people are so good at goal setting, and so lousy at goal getting. This is also why New Year's resolutions for the most part are an absolute waste of time.

Keep It Positive

Make certain all your goals are set in the positive. If you say, "I will not yell at my kids today," your mind will think more about yelling. Instead, if you think, "I will maintain a calm, peaceful, loving spirit today," you are apt to be more effective in your pursuit. Sitting and watching my boys' baseball games, I often hear the other parents yelling at our pitcher, "Don't lose this batter!" It takes no more effort to say, "Let's get this one!" or "Let's strike this one out!" Instead of "Don't strike out!" why not say, "Let's get a hit!" One is positive, the other is negative. Focusing on the positive empowers us, focusing on the negative disempowers or drains us. Setting goals for balance requires a positive focus.

setting Goals For Balance

Since goal setting is the process of planting the seeds of our dreams, it would seem logical that in order to live a balanced life, we need to set balanced goals as a first step toward the realization of our dreams. For some strange reason, many people have balanced dreams but set imbalanced goals. The first step toward realizing your dream of a happy home life is setting goals in that arena of your life. The dream of owing your own home will begin to come to reality when you take the first step and set a goal to save $100 each month for the down payment. The dream of being debt-free begins to come to fruition the moment you set the goal to take specific action. Wherever we plant, we pick.

Let's look at planting seeds in the five areas that can bring Real Balance to our lives. Start by getting five pieces of paper and write one of each of the five "F" words across the top, i.e., Family Dreams. The next step is to turn your dreams into goals.

setting Faith Goals

As we set goals in the areas of our fitness, our family, our friends and our finances, we are setting goals that will require faith to act upon. Without faith we can't achieve our goals, we remain inactive *goal setters* instead of *goal getters*. Think of it. Why would we take the risk if we didn't have faith in our ability to achieve? Faith goals can help you achieve a state of spiritual well-being. A state of mind that says: "I can do *all* things!" Not alone, but with the help of those around me, and the power of the Creator living within me.

Here are some ideas for faith goals.

Faith in Myself
- constant positive self-talk
- list your assets (count your blessings)
- daily positive affirmations
- review past successes monthly (remind yourself of your wins)
- go on a mission trip (you'll believe you really can make a difference)
- empower and enrich others

Faith in Others
- share goals
- let others help

Faith in God
- prayer time
- meditation
- Bible study
- church attendance

Once your faith goals are set, it's time to take a look at setting some fitness goals to build the mind and body you will need to achieve all your other goals.

Setting Fitness Goals

Again, if we don't feel well, what else matters? Unless you are feeling energized physically and mentally, it is going be very difficult to set goals and achieve success in the other areas of your life. Your overall goal needs to be a state of wellness in mind and body. Think of your body as the hardware, and your mind as the software. To operate at maximum efficiency, both require regular upgrading. Just ask Bill Gates. Think of setting fitness goals as upgrading your hardware and your software.

Mental
- languages you will learn
- building your vocabulary
- books you will read
- tapes you will listen to

- hobbies
- thoughts you will dwell on
- words you will speak

Physical

- diet
- water
- exercise
- relaxation
- vacation
- physical weight and shape
- sleep routine
- breathing
- bad habit replacements

Once you've completed a list of at least 10 fitness goals, it's time to move on to setting goals in the area of our life that the majority of us say is the most important, our family.

Setting Family Goals

To set your family goals, start by reviewing the dreams you have for your family. These are the relationships with the special people in our lives that are part of our family. Many times we look at our dreams, and have no idea where to begin turning that dream into a goal. When I teach my goal setting seminars I give my audience a list of joggers to help them with the process, and most times inspire new dreams as well. I believe they could be helpful for you too. Here they are.

Spouse Goals

- daily shared time
- weekly date
- yearly honeymoon

Children Goals

- daily shared time
- education
- sports
- devotional opportunities

Parent and Sibling Goals

- regular visits
- phone calls
- cards
- family reunions
- forgiveness

Once you've written out at least 10 family goals, it's now time to move on to setting some friend goals. Goals that determine to a great degree what other life goals we set, and the type of person we become in the process.

Setting Friend Goals

We've all heard it: "It's not what you know, but who you know." This is especially true of our *inner circle*. These friends, as a group, are a key factor in our quest for Real Balance. It is virtually impossible for us to remain balanced if our inner circle friends are not and see no value in it. Here are some friend goal ideas:

- daily phone call or e-mail of encouragement to a friend
- a weekly card of appreciation
- entertain guests in your home once a month
- create a mastermind team
- associate with positive, optimistic people
- look for people you would like to meet
- think about friendships you'd like to initiate
- set a daily hug quota

Now that you have set your friend goals, you are ready to set goals for the area of your career, your business and your money. Your financial goals.

Setting Financial Goals

- get a raise
- secure a promotion
- start a business
- begin a new career

- spend 15 minutes a day reading something relating to your career/business
- increase annual earnings from business
- real estate investments
- retirement savings
- registered educational savings plan
- bank account balance
- recording all expenses
- debt reduction
- giving money
- giving time
- sharing your knowledge

Congratulations—if you wrote down just five goals in each of the five areas, you already have more written goals than 97 percent of the people around you. You are now ready to move on to the process of *getting* your goals.

PRioRiTiZE YoUR GoalS

An old German proverb says, "He who begins too much accomplishes little." How true! Some of us have a greater ability to manage multiple projects than others. Before moving on, prioritize your goals by writing a number beside each of them, with 1 being most important to you and 10 being the least important to you, if you've listed 10 goals. It's easy to focus on one goal at a time; it's more challenging to focus on 10 at a time!

In fact, it is impossible to focus on more than one thing at a time. That does not mean, however, that it is impossible to achieve more than one goal at a time. It most certainly is possible. It's called killing two birds with one stone. Sometimes it can be three or four. For example, if two of your goals were to exercise daily and to spend time with your family every day, you could take your family for walks together. Or, if it were daily exercise, daily solitude and daily prayer time, you could do all three at once, and still be focusing only on your prayer. You get the drift.

Getting Goals

As you can see, getting goals is a process, a process that begins with a dream. That dream is a visualization of a desired outcome or result. It is the visualization of a harvest. The next step is to turn your dream into a goal by putting it in writing, and then prioritizing and determining which goals you will work on first. This is where we develop an action plan and take action on our goals. This is where we move beyond believing it's possible, to find the faith that it's probable. This is what gives feet to our goals and they start to come to fruition. It gives them much more than a deadline, it gives them a lifeline.

THROW Me a Lifeline

Most of us are aware that in order for a goal to be a goal, it must be clearly stated in writing. The other thing we've been told is that every goal needs a deadline in order to be effective, in order for us not to procrastinate on taking action toward the achievement of it. I agree, deadlines can be an effective means of communicating to others the timeframe in which they must complete the task, or they're dead! However, when it comes to our own goals, deadlines are the cause of a lot of negative stress, and the death of many goals. What goals need much more than deadlines are lifelines.

Here is what I mean by a lifeline:

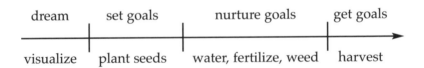

dream	set goals		nurture goals	get goals
visualize	plant seeds		water, fertilize, weed	harvest

In order to keep our goals alive and growing, they need to be nurtured. Nurturing our goals can happen in many ways. It's identifying the resources we need before we take action. It's being willing to pay the price in order to reap the rewards. It's making sure our goals remain congruent with our values and our purpose. It's the process of regular review of our goals and priorities. It's the updating of progress and making adjustments to our course if required. It's ignoring the negative comments of those who want to rain on our parade, instead of getting one of their own. It can be the encouragement of those friends who believe in us and want us to succeed.

RecaPPinG

- Dream without limits (think big!).
- Believe that all things are possible.
- Set goals that are achievable, but make you stretch.
- Write goals clearly and in a way they can be measured.
- Share your goals with those who will support you.
- State all goals in the positive.
- Set faith goals.
- Set fitness goals.
- Set family goals.
- Set friend goals.
- Set financial goals.
- Give your goals a *lifeline.*
- Nurture them to maturity.
- Go for it!

Eliminate the time between the idea and the act, and your dreams will become realities.

FinDinG TiMe FoR iT ALL

How thin can you spread yourself, before you're no longer there?

In a world where "too much to do and too little time" is a common mantra, there's a felt sense that everyone else has more control over their day than we do. While we may be at the beck and call of everyone from our clients to our boss, there are still areas where the culprit is none other than ourselves.

In order to bring balance and a sense of control to your life, this chapter will suggest some ways you can begin to gain some relief from self-induced pressure. This sense of control will reduce the stress in your life and help you have more fun at everything you do.

Can THe CLUTTeR

Get rid of the clutter. Do you walk into your office and instantly feel a sense you could be buried in the mess? Papers are piled on the desk, on the floor, and the stack of magazines on your credenza continues to grow higher. Yesterday's mail is buried under today's. Memos and messages are everywhere. Some people need to have every file in sight that they've worked on over the past five years. They use a *piling system* instead of a *filing system*. But for most people clutter only wastes a lot of time when it comes to finding what you need. No wonder you are spending so many hours at the office. Searching through stacks of papers is no one's definition of being efficient.

Before you can even think of setting up procedures that will keep you organized, you must clean up the mess. Here's how you can get rid of the clutter real quickly. Grab four envelope boxes and label them Priority, Routine, Junk Mail and Magazines. Now before you take another call or do anything else throw everything on your desk into one of those four boxes. What a great feeling it is to have a clean desk. Now take the Priority box and start dispensing with the items one at a time. Stick with it. It may take a couple of hours but pick from the bottom of the pile. Always deal with the top piece of paper first and throw away any excess paper. When you get to your Magazine box, rip out the stories you plan to read later and toss the rest.

Getting Organized

The next step to getting organized is to develop a simple follow-up system. This has been a real lifesaver for me. Grab 13 hanging file folders and label them January, February and so on, through to December. The last file is labeled Next Year. Then take 31 file folders and label them 1 to 31. These go into the desk drawer closest to your phone. Every morning you simply remove the contents of the file for that day and then replace the folder into next month's folder. In that file are not only the reminders for the follow-up calls but also the previous correspondence. Not only the notice for remittances and payments due, but also a copy of the statement, form or invoice. What a time saver!

Once you begin to save time, it is important not to let others steal the time you've saved. Learn to say NO, not now, not ever. Learn to say it with a smile. If you don't put limits on your time, it can be stolen with your unknowing permission. Have a quiet time every morning. This is a time when you are available only to yourself. Close your door and don't take calls. This is your time to think and plan.

When you plan your day, select the highest priorities from your To Do list and schedule a time in your planner when you will complete them. Make an appointment with yourself to complete the tasks. Otherwise, you'll waste a lot of time every day rewriting To Do lists. Even schedule a time to deal with your mail rather than dropping everything when it arrives just to browse. Pick up each piece of paper only once. Follow the six "D"s of paper handling:

MaNaGiNG YᵒUR MaiL

Discard it. If you can do without it, get rid of it. This can be junk mail or any mail that does not require a response. Chuck it!

Delegate it. If someone else can act upon it, delegate it. Record this in your delegation binder or you may forget what you've assigned to others.

Do it. If it's important and can be done quickly, just do it! If it's a letter or a fax, jot your response across the bottom and send it back by fax or mail. No need to waste stationery in most cases.

Develop it. If it's important, can only be done by you, but will take longer than 15 minutes, schedule a time to complete it. Then drop that piece of paper into the follow-up file for the day you have scheduled to do it. That way it's off your desk and you'll find it when you need it.

Delay it. If it needs to be done by you, but it's not a priority, delay it by adding it to your To Do list. When you have a spare moment, work away at it.

Deposit it. If paperwork must be retained for future reference, file it, or deposit it in a 3-ring binder for easy retrieval. An organized filing system is the beginning of an organized life.

JUSt Dᵒ It!

Getting organized is a real challenge for most people. The reason, as you probably noticed thus far, is the time we need to get ourselves organized. It's the old chicken-egg syndrome. Take a look at your office. Is the layout efficient, or do you waste a lot of time walking to get files and use equipment? Then, take a look at your home. What about your garage? If you've been procrastinating with getting organized, don't put it off. The best time to start is now!

Perhaps what you need to get started is a Daily Routine Chart. A schedule that makes time for all that is important to you. A tool to help keep you on track. This chart can be customized to fit your career and lifestyle.

Daily Routine Chart

 RENEWAL — 10:00 P.M. TO 6:00 A.M.

- Start your day the night before. Get enough restful sleep. If you only need 7 hours, take a half-hour off either end of this period. If we observe nature, we will notice deepening silence and calm throughout the environment as night falls. If we allow it in, this settling, calming effect will be reflected in our bodies; as a result it will prepare our bodies for sleep.

POWER HOUR — 6:00 A.M. TO 7:00 A.M.

- Wake up not much later than 6:00 a.m. You can gradually teach yourself to do this without an alarm clock.
- Drink a glass of warm water to moisten your vocal cords and to stimulate your gastrointestinal system and encourage a bowel movement.
- Do 5 minutes of stretching exercises.
- Practice breathing exercise and meditation.
- Walk or jog for 20 minutes.
- Spend 10 minutes reading and praying.
- Shower using warm water. Not hot or cold.
- Make lunches for the kids on school days.
- Gently wake the kids and invite them to join you for breakfast.
- Eat a light breakfast. Skip the fried potatoes, sausages and bacon.

MAKING HAY — 7:00 A.M. TO NOON

- If you commute to work, make the most of travel time by listening to tapes that will educate, motivate and inspire you. Make your driving time, mental exercise time. Learn a new language, a new skill. The possibilities are endless.
- If you work in an office, first check your e-mail, faxes and voice mail.

- Make the next 60 to 90 minutes your quiet hour and work on high-priority tasks.
- From 10:00 a.m. to 12:00 noon, schedule appointments, meetings, correspondence and calls.

REFUELLING — NOON TO 1:00 P.M.

- Eat an early lunch; this should be the largest meal of the day; avoid rushing or eating at your desk.
- Take a few moments to sit quietly, then walk for 5 to 15 minutes to help with your digestion.
- If you're over 50, take a 20-minute nap.

BACK AT IT — 1:00 P.M. TO 6:00 P.M.

- If you work in an office, first check your e-mail, faxes and voice mail.
- From 1:30 p.m. to 3:30 p.m., schedule appointments and complete priority tasks
- For the last hour and a half, schedule meetings and make phone calls
- If you commute, use the drive home to listen to relaxing music and unwind

FAMILY TIME — 6:00 P.M. TO 8:00 P.M.

- Eat a moderate dinner.
- Sit quietly for a few moments after eating, do the dishes and then take a short walk to help with digestion.
- Engage in a family activity with your children if they are still at home, like playing baseball, playing games or just wrestling on the floor.
- Call parents and siblings.
- Tuck in the children.

"ME" TIME — 8:00 P.M. TO 10:00 P.M.

- Read.
- Relax.
- Call friends to stay in touch.
- Go for a walk with your spouse if you have one.
- Bedtime should be at least three hours after dinner. Don't read, eat or watch television in bed. If you keep the bed reserved for sleep-related activities you'll have less trouble with insomnia. Instead of lying in bed awake, your brain will trigger sleep when you hit the pillow. Good night. Sweet dreams.

No matter how well we schedule our day it still seems challenging to make time for keeping our bodies physically fit. Sometimes we just need to "think outside the box" and create the space we never knew we had.

FinDing Time to Exercise

Finding the time to exercise is often as much of a challenge as your new aerobic workout itself. In fact, the number one reason given for not exercising is lack of time. That's why it's so important to have a regular exercise schedule. One that lets you know where and when you're planning to work out each week. Of course, plans can change. But it's better to skip an exercise session because of a higher priority conflict than to have no schedule at all. If you save your workouts for whenever a spare moment pops up, you'll end up exercising infrequently. Intermittent exercise increases your risk of injury because the muscles, bones and tendons can receive too much stress, too soon.

Your own schedule might involve a variety of workout times— morning workouts on some days, for example; lunchtime or after-work exercise sessions on other days. The key is to find a blend that works for you, and stick with it. You may prefer an early morning workout, since you can shower afterward and get on with your working day. When you get out of bed, spend 15 to 20 minutes relaxing, reading and feeding your mind before you begin your exercise session. This gives your body a chance to shake off the effects of sleep. Be sure to warm up fully by stretching your muscles at the beginning of each workout.

If walking or biking is your favorite aerobic exercise, and you don't perspire so heavily you have to shower after a light workout, then walking or cycling to work can be another way of fitting in some aerobic exercise. Simply wear athletic shoes and keep an extra pair of dress shoes at the office. Or bring a pair of athletic shoes to work, and fit in a walk on the way home. The other option is to take your car, bus or subway only part of the way to work if it's too far to walk all the way. Then walk back to that point on the way home. You'll be more relaxed when you arrive home and your family time will be much more enjoyable. For them and for you.

If you do not work outside the home or you are self-employed and working from your home, you might enjoy breaking up the day with a workout break. Instead of taking a 20-minute break to read the paper or have a snack, stretch your break a few minutes longer, enjoy a 45-minute walk, bicycle ride or swim, or put a favorite aerobic exercise tape in your VCR. You'll find an exercise break is even more relaxing than putting up your feet.

Lunchtime can be a good time for a 45-minute walk, cycle or swim. If you're a swimmer or prefer the facilities of a health club, your pool or club should be close to your place of business. You'll probably need a least an hour for this type of workout, by the time you get in and change and do the same on the way out.

If you get ready for church before the rest of your family, start walking and have them pick you up on the way. I do that regularly. It gives me time alone to think, pray and exercise. If you're going out for dinner with your spouse, start walking as soon as you're ready instead of sitting down in front of the TV. Either way, make sure to tell the driver which route you will be taking so they will find you on the way!

Finally, unless you're nine months pregnant and have six kids with you under the age of 6, don't use the drive-thru window when stopping for a bite to eat when you're on the road. Park as far as you can from the door and race your kids for it. The last one there buys; usually it's dad.

One Stone, Two Birds

As mentioned earlier, many times we can achieve more than one goal with same activity. No, I'm not talking about driving, reading the newspaper and talking on the cell phone at the same time. There are ways to safely complete one activity and be moving toward three or four goals at the same time. This is the ultimate time saver. It is a simple concept, but the payoff is incredible. Here's an example of how you can save time by achieving more than one goal via a single activity.

Let's say four of your goals were as follows:

- Exercise daily
- Spend time daily in solitude
- Spend time every day in prayer
- Spend time with nature daily

There is no tomorrow.

You could achieve all four goals with one activity by taking a walk alone in the woods every morning. Take a look at your goals and activities to see which activities could perhaps be slightly altered. There are so many possibilities. For instance, I take my boys to their baseball games, but before the game starts, while they are practicing, my wife Elizabeth and I go for a walk. That one activity of taking the boys to their ball games meets the following goals, all at the same time:

- Spending time my family
- Spending time with my spouse

- Getting my physical exercise
- Meeting new people (the other parents at the game)

Recapping

- Get out of bed not much later than 6:00 a.m., earlier if you can.
- Listen to audiotapes while you drive.
- Have a quiet hour every day.
- Get rid of the clutter.
- Set up an efficient filing system.
- Start using a follow-up system.
- Handle mail only once.
- Throw out stuff you don't need.
- Tear out the pages of interest from your magazines and throw out the rest.
- Phone instead of writing.
- Take a book along to read when you're traveling or waiting in the dentist's office.
- Get proficient with latest technology. E-mail can save time and money.
- Delegate where practical.
- Be achieving more than one goal with the same activity.
- Spend less time in front of the television.
- Develop a daily routine. Have your own rituals of balance.

"The average person only has about 300 months left to live. Let us spend this time as carefully as we would spend our last 300 dollars."

Gary W. Fenchuck

Making Change Happen

"It's hard for me to get used to these changing times.
I can remember when the air was clean and sex was
dirty."

George Burns

With so much talk about change recently, I was going to avoid the use of the word altogether in this book. Then I realized that would be ridiculous, because nothing happens without change. Nothing changes, until something changes. Somehow we tend to think of change as something undesirable, something initiated by another person, and it can be. But change can also be wonderful, exciting and initiated by us.

Just think about how exciting change was to you as a child. A new brother or sister, a new school, a new bicycle, new friends, new clothes. As children, change meant excitement. We were flexible, we were open to change—we had to be, and we were still growing. Perhaps that's why most adults are so resistant to change, so inflexible—because they have stopped growing. Without change a seed could not become a flower. Without change there would be no seasons. You've likely heard it before, but it bears repeating: "The definition of insanity: doing the same thing, but expecting different results."

Most of us are looking for different results in some area of our lives. Or, for some of us, in all areas of our lives. Different results or a different outcome means essentially a different harvest. In order to reap a different harvest, we must change the kind of seed we're planting. This concept is based on the laws of the harvest found in the number-one best-selling book of all time, the Bible.

THe Laws of THe Harvest

For more than 20 years now I have studied the lives of people who appeared to be successful and those who seemed to be losers. Some of these people were born into poverty, but became very wealthy. While others who were born into wealth, ended up in the poorhouse. Some had little or no formal education, but became very wise individuals. While others spent most of their lives in school, but seemed to act as though they were fools. However, the one thing all the successful people, whose lives I studied, seemed to have in common was this: an understanding of a set of universal and timeless principals called the *laws of the harvest*.

The laws of the harvest are found in Galations 6:7 "Be not deceived, God is not mocked: For whatsoever a man soweth, that shall he also reap." Simple, but profound, these few words contain the keys to success in every area of our lives. The laws of the harvest have no respect for age, financial status or religious belief. They can be our greatest asset or our greatest liability. Much like the law of gravity, they can help or hinder us. The choice is ours. We get to choose the seeds we plant into our minds, the soil of our lives.

As I studied this verse further I realized it contained seven important laws that determine success or failure in *every* area of our lives.

THe seven Laws of THe Harvest

1. You pick what you plant, but usually a whole lot more.
2. Planting always comes before harvest.
3. Every seed must die before it can reproduce.
4. You don't need to plant seeds to get weeds.
5. There's a season to sow and a season to reap.
6. The risk is always the greatest just before harvest.
7. Keep planting if you want to keep reaping.

Let's take a closer look at how the seven laws of the harvest apply to all areas of our lives. These laws determine whether we will reap a bountiful crop of happiness, love and material abundance, or a crop of weeds (misery, anxiety, depression and greed).

1. You pick what you plant, but usually a whole lot more.
This seems to be so obvious. If it is, why does it come as a surprise to so many people who have been consumed by a career or business for years to discover they have lost their family shortly after they've found financial success. Or, they discover they've lost their soul in the process. Others treat people dishonestly and wonder why the rest of the world cheats them.

They eat junk foods, never take a break and fail to get proper exercise, then wonder why they have heart attacks, become obese or lack energy and enthusiasm. They abuse their bodies with tobacco and are shocked to discover they have cancer cells growing inside them. What goes around, comes around! What we sow, we reap. Not only that, one seed of corn produces a whole cob of corn, sometimes two.

Our mind, as well, only grows the kind of crops that are planted in it. If you plant a seed of doubt, you will reap a crop of fear. Plant a seed of fear, and you will reap a crop of the very thing you fear. The thing you fear usually comes upon you. However, if you plant the seeds of faith in your mind, you can expect to reap the very thing you are believing. Believe it, and you *will* see it.

If you want a bountiful crop, plant plenty of seeds. Abundant reaping requires abundant sowing. If you want lots of hugs, you need to give lots of hugs away. If you would like your financial needs abundantly met, freely give to those in need. Do you want a friend? Then be a friend. Do you want to be happier? Then start making others happy!

A farmer decides in the spring what crop it is he would like to harvest later that year. He cannot change his mind and harvest a crop he did not plant. So it is in your personal life. Your harvest is determined at the time of planting, not at the time of harvest. Your future depends on the seeds you are planting today. If you want love and respect from your kids when they are teenagers or adults, give them your time and effort today, before they are grown up and it's too late.

Enjoying a healthy body in the future will be determined by how you look after your body today. Regularly plant seeds of physical exercise, a healthy diet and adequate sleep and you will reap a life of wellness instead of disease.

When we sow the seeds of love, integrity and balance in our lives, then fertilize them with passion, enthusiasm and a positive mental attitude, we reap a harvest of Total Prosperity.

2. Planting always comes before harvest.

Sounds like common sense, but I don't find common sense to be all that common. Too many people expect a harvest before they plant any seeds. They plan to plant after they've reaped enough to satisfy all their needs. They will start giving to charity after they have paid off the mortgage and have put the kids through college. They will begin volunteering their time once they're not so busy with their careers or businesses. They'll be a friend after you first become one to them. They will work harder and longer and take more responsibility after they receive that raise in pay. To think you can harvest before you plant doesn't make any sense!

A dream is a visualization of the achievement of a goal. It is not a goal. Before a dream can become a goal it must be put in writing. This act of writing down our goals is how we plant seeds in our lives. Just as planting comes before reaping, goal setting as comes before goal getting.

Just as our feelings are the crop we reap as a result of the actions we have sown, our actions are the result of the seeds of thought we have planted in our past. This principle applies to any harvest. The planting of the seed must take place first.

The keys to reaping a harvest of success in every area of your life are, first, plan your crop—dream your dreams; second, prepare the soil—define the resources required to reach your goals; third, plant the seed—write down your goals; fourth, maintain the soil—guard your thoughts; last, get your goals—reap your crop.

3. Every seed must die before it can reproduce.

The sower takes the risk and plants the seed, but he cannot make it grow. As we invest ourselves in the lives of people around us, we take a risk. Sowing seeds of love and affection, we invest hugely and risk never seeing that love returned by the person we may be helping at the time. After we've done our part...sometimes all we can do is believe. Like the farmer, we just keep on planting in faith *knowing* God gives the increase and we *will* eventually reap what we have sown.

Our faith in God is the moisture our seeds require in order to germinate. It takes a lot of faith to plant something knowing it must die and we may never see it again, but the risk is worth the rewards. Without death, there is no life. Without the possibility of loss, there can be no win. Without valleys, there could be no mountains. Without sorrow, there would be no joy!

When we experience crop failures (and we will), they can be our worst *and* best experiences. They make us better, stronger and wiser. There are no failures in life—only learning experiences. Failures can be fertilizer that helps us grow, or deadly chemicals that destroy our lives. The choice is ours! Think about these people:

- Walt Disney was fired by a newspaper editor for a lack of ideas. Walt Disney also went bankrupt several times before he built Disneyland.
- Babe Ruth, one of the greatest athletes of all time and famous for setting the home run record, also holds the record for strike-outs.
- Henry Ford went broke five times before he finally became a success.

4. You don't need to plant seeds to get weeds.

Weeds seem to grow as though they had been planted by an unseen hand. This seems to happen as well in our own lives; unless we are continually sowing and cultivating the seeds of love, the weeds of envy and hate will begin to grow. Continually feeding our minds with positive information will prevent the negativism from sprouting and shooting up, bearing a crop of weeds. If we're always making a positive impact on our families by sowing into their lives the seeds of caring, sharing and leading by example, we can be sure that their lives will bear a bountiful harvest, free of weeds.

We are what we are because of the seeds that have been sown in our minds, the people we've met and the influence those people have had on our lives. Positive, happy, successful people feed their minds with that which is uplifting, positive, good and pure. They also choose to associate with other people who are positive and prosperous. This is planting good seeds.

People who have failed miserably at life have fed their minds with bad news and negative self-talk. They love to talk about their problems and those of others. They love to criticize and put down, instead of building up their fellow workers. The seeds they plant are weed seeds, and weeds are the crop they reap.

In my life, I think of weed seeds as the negative thoughts that want to keep planting themselves into my mind. If these negative thoughts are not rejected immediately, they begin to choke out the good, happy and positive thoughts. The weeds that grow are the bad habits we form. Good seeds grow into good habits. Every seed becomes a habit that either helps or hinders us. An act repeated, or seed that is nurtured and maintained for 21 to 30 days, becomes a *habit*. This period of time is the gestation period for a habit, provided the conditions are right.

Maintenance requires continually monitoring our motives, desires and needs. Weeding our garden means going through it and deciding which plants are weeds, then removing them so they can no longer grow. Weeding our minds is much the same process; however, instead of weeding plants, we must weed out our critical, negative thoughts. We cannot stop some seeds from falling into our minds but it's our choice whether we let them take root or not.

Maintenance also requires the fertilizing of our good, pure, positive thoughts with a regular daily review of our goals, reading good books and listening to tapes that inspire, motivate and educate.

5. There's a season to sow and a season to reap.

Each of our lives is made up of seasons. A season to be born, a season to die. There is a season when we care for our children and then there comes a season when they care for us. There is a season to sow and a season to reap.

It took seven years of burning the candle at both ends before I burnt out. It also took six months of applying balanced living principles before I really noticed a significant change in my physical, mental and spiritual condition, and a full year before I felt completely restored. Even though I did experience a positive change in my condition before the end of the six months, the "up times" didn't last long and were followed by bouts of depression.

The abuse of their bodies with alcohol, tobacco, drugs, lack of exercise, a poor diet or workaholism during their youth is the reason many people spend their so-called "golden years" in poor health. After spending a lifetime working toward retirement, they arrive only to find misery, boredom and sickness. Unwittingly, many people exchange a full and long life for a few years of the "good times," (if you can call abuse of our bodies "good times"), followed by sickness and premature death.

It may take a while, but we always reap what we sow. We may not see the harvest as soon as we sow the seed, but it will grow. It will multiply. It's the law of the harvest—a universal, timeless, natural law!

6. The risk is always the greatest just before harvest.

It's always darkest just before sunrise and the risk is always greatest just before harvest. If you are about to give up, this law should be of great encouragement to you. Our investment and our risk are greatest just before harvest. After the farmer plants the seed, he must continue investing time and money in his crop, cultivating and fertilizing it. As the investment increases, so does the risk. If you have been planting and praying or maintaining, *don't quit*! Your crop could be just about to burst through the ground—you could be giving up on the brink of a miracle.

7. Keep planting if you want to keep reaping.

Sowing must become a lifestyle for each one of us. When it does, we can call ourselves *sowers*. In life, it seems that it's the sowers who seem to be given all the seed. It's no wonder they also seem to get all the harvest. Therefore, a sower can't be caught without seed. Any farmer knows well that if he fed all of his grain to his livestock and didn't save any seed for the next spring's planting, he couldn't expect a crop. Similarly, if he didn't have the resources with which to buy seed, he couldn't very well hope to have a harvest that fall.

In most lives, consuming the entire harvest is the norm rather than the exception, yet we wonder why there is no crop for us to harvest. We fail to plant by failing to take some of the love we receive and sowing it into the lives of those we meet. We eventually find ourselves without friends and living very lonely lives. We can reap a financial harvest by taking a portion of the money we earn and investing it in a worthy cause.

Every seed contains the full-blown flower.

However, in most cases, we feel justified in not helping someone because of our own financial state of affairs. So we use our money to pay off the mortgage or car loan and, before we know it, there is *no* seed left to sow, money to give, time to contribute or love to share. It is important to consider the seed portion of any harvest as high priority and set it aside so it is available for planting when the season arrives or the opportunity arises.

Start planting good seeds today. It's easy to know what seeds to plant—just plant what it is that you want to reap. Remember, the amount you reap is determined by the amount you sow! To reap a bountiful harvest, we must sow good seeds generously, in faith, believing that we will reap. You will reap whatever you sow, in every area of your life.

CHANGE — OR BE CHANGED

Consider practicing change on your own; that way it won't be as scary when it happens when you are not expecting it. Here are some ideas for changes that you can initiate on your own:

- Make changes in the area of your friends if you have some who should be replaced.
- Take a different route to work tomorrow.
- Change your career if you don't *love* it.
- Take a computer course and upgrade your skills.
- Change the way you wake up in the morning.
- Change the way you wake up your children. Try singing.
- Change your diet. Fast for a day.
- Change your vocabulary. Learn one new word a day.
- Change your attitude.
- Change your fitness routine.
- Take a vacation to a spot you've never visited.
- Change churches if you're not happy with yours.
- Take business courses to prepare for possible downsizing that may result in your becoming an entrepreneur involuntarily.
- Change your television viewing habits.

The more we prepare for and practice change, the less traumatic and stressful unexpected change will be. Sometimes we have to give up the good in order to get the best.

> **"We cannot become what we need to be by remaining what we are."**
>
> Max DePree

PART FOUR:
STAYING ON TRACK

"For every mile of road, there's two miles of ditch."

Neil Aitcheson

STaYiNG ENERGiZED

"Most people give up just when they're about to achieve success. They quit on the one-yard line. They give up at the last minute of the game, one foot from the winning touchdown."

H. Ross Perot

A Little PUSH

A wealthy businessman hosted a spectacular party during which he filled his swimming pool with sharks, barracuda and other assorted dangerous fish. He then announced to his guests that he would like to challenge any one of them to try swimming across the pool. To the first person to swim the length of the pool, he offered as first prize a choice of the following: a trip around the world, a new home in the mountains or the position of president of his company.

No sooner had he finished making the announcement, and there was a big splash in the pool and a young man began to swim at lightning speed through the shark-infested water. As he leaped out of the water at the other end, the millionaire approached the dripping and shaking young man and said, "That was a stunning performance. You are a very brave person. Which prize do you choose?" The swimmer caught his breath and then replied, "Right now I really don't care about the prize. I just want to find out who the person was that pushed me in!"

Many times when we are feeling discouraged, like we don't have the energy to go on, all we need is a little push to get us moving. We often rely on external motivators to get us started. We look for others to motivate us. But the secret is to learn to generate the push from within. To be energized and motivated on a daily basis, you learn to motivate yourself. It all begins by giving yourself a prize to work toward. The prizes are the rewards for reaching the goals you've set for yourself. If you skipped over the chapter on goal setting without writing any down, do it now. This act in itself will bring a boost of energy.

Goals

The number one cause of depression is the lack of clearly defined, long-term goals. Have you ever seen a depressed person bursting with energy? Have you ever had a depressed person passionately share their goals? Not a chance. The first key to getting energized is to regularly set clearly defined goals. The first key to staying energized is to review them regularly. Keep them handy for a quick review when you get a moment, stuck in traffic or whatever. However, it does take more than goals to keep restoring this renewable resource in bodies called energy. This chapter is about keeping our energy at optimum level in order for us to accomplish the goals that we have set for our lives. It's about enthusiasm for life itself.

Enthusiasm

Enthusiasm is like a magnet that draws people to you. It's infectious, and people enjoy being around it. Enthusiasm is getting so excited about what you are doing that other people can't help but want to do it with you. In the words of Ralph Waldo Emerson, "Nothing great is achieved without enthusiasm."

Many people never come to realize the tremendous power and incredible energy behind enthusiasm. It reflects confidence, raises morale and spreads good cheer. It also inspires those around us. Those with whom you come in contact will always feel your enthusiastic approach to life. Everyone is attracted to the magnetism of enthusiasm. Andrew Carnegie stated, "Enthusiasm is a great leavening force in the mental world, for it gives power to purpose. It helps free your mind of negative influences and brings you peace of mind. Lastly, it inspires personal initiative, both in thought and physical action."

It is difficult to be enthusiastic without feeling energetic. You can never do your best unless you are enthusiastic. There are sources of energy all around us; all we need to do is tap into them. These sources of energy are available to anyone who takes the initiative to reach out for them.

Environment

Our friends either energize us or drain us. Think about it, some people leave your presence and it seems they just sucked the life out of you. Other friends listen to your goals and encourage you to achieve them; they compliment and praise you, they motivate you and they energize you. When they leave your presence, you feel like you could take on the world. They make you feel better about yourself. They make you feel more positive about everything. Your obstacles look a lot smaller. You're ready for anything. Friends are part of our environment. Choose them carefully—our environment determines how we think.

The thoughts we think every day have an incredible impact on our level of energy. It is our thoughts that ignite the fuel we put into our bodies. If our thoughts are negative, nothing happens; if they are positive, the sparks fly. The thoughts we think are determined by environment and our friends are part of that environment, but there's more to environment than friends. Our place of employment is part of our environment. Are your co-workers positive people, who share your values? Do you have fun at your job? Are you excited about going to work every morning? If you don't love it, leave! A new job can be the first step to changing your environment.

Love It or Leave It

When my brother Pete (who is 11 months younger than I am and has twice as much hair) left the Farm at the age of 16, he attended a community college to get his high school equivalency diploma and then got a job with the railway. A job that paid enough to support him, his wife and one child, but had little future in terms of growth. I began to correspond with Pete from the Farm since I was still there, and began to encourage him to take up the electrical trade. His response would always be, "How can I take a pay cut from $10 to $6, even though I know it's temporary. I couldn't make ends meet." He sounded trapped! He was sounding like the rest of his co-workers, I'm sure. I was determined to do my part, so I went out and bought Pete a tool pouch and filled it with all the tools he would need as an electrician apprentice and mailed it to him with an encouraging note. I hoped it was the *push* he needed.

It was! The pay cut was short-lived when Pete's new employer realized what a fantastic worker and brilliant individual he was. Within six months he was back to earning the same pay he had left, and within three years he was a licensed electrician earning 50 percent more than the job he left, and loving it! The most amazing part of the story is what happened to Pete's attitude when he changed his work environment. His new career eventually led to working with people who had higher values. People with a different vocabulary. People with spiritual values. Pete started attending church with his family. What a miracle to see a life transformed by a change in environment!

Doing what you love is also a tremendous energizer! Many times after I've spoken to an audience people will come up to me and say, "Where do you get all the energy? You looked like were loving every minute on stage." I do. That is why I have so much energy when I'm up there. One gentleman in his sixties came up to me after a speech and said, "Wow, I feel like I just did a 45-minute workout watching you share your message. You were so passionate." He's right, passion is powerful. Passion energizes not only ourselves, but also those around us.

Honey, I'm Home

It's sometimes our home environment not our work environment, that drains our energy. Instead of coming home to a haven of rest, we come home to an atmosphere of conflict and stress. Someone once said, "No wonder dog is man's best friend! When he gets home the dog stops whatever it's doing, runs up to his master, wags his tail and fetches the paper." Do you stop what you what you're doing for two minutes to greet your spouse, when he or she arrives home? What about even 20 seconds, to hug and set the stage for a relaxing evening?

If your home is a haven of peace and rest, you will have a lot more energy to face the following day. That is, providing you will eat and exercise properly while you are there. Let's say you come home after a long day at the office and everything is peaceful and quiet, and you eat a big greasy meal after you've had a couple of beers. You then top off your dinner with a big slice of apple pie à la mode, then lie down on the couch. You reach for a pack of cigarettes and watch television for the evening. I can guarantee, you won't feel very energetic. I'm sure you can tell by now that to feel energetic, you must do what energetic people do. Remember that the feeling always follows the act, not vice versa.

Eat Like a Rabbit

Enough of how *not* to eat. You may be sick and tired of hearing about nutrition, but without the right nutrients your body will not have energy. Nutrients are the fuel our minds and bodies need to perform. To have a high-performance body, you must fuel it with high-octane fuel. Just think about rabbits, they eat a lot of greens. They also have a lot of energy, and enjoy an active sex life! The nutrients you take in, combined with the proper fitness, rest and lifestyle, determine the amount of energy you put out.

The two primary sources of energy when it comes to food are fat and glycogen (a usable chemical form of sugar found in the blood resulting from the breakdown of carbohydrates). Protein provides little energy, but is required for cellular and tissue repair and growth.

Well, what are carbohydrates? They are high-octane foods that provide the fastest form of energy to our body. These are high-performance foods. However, there are two kinds of carbohydrates. There are simple carbohydrates and there are complex carbohydrates. Both provide glucose, but complex carbohydrates provide several nutritional advantages: vitamins, minerals and fiber. The most common complex carbohydrate is called starch, which is found in beans, vegetables, grains and fruit. Here's list of high-octane or energy foods:

- Bread, crackers, pitas, pretzels, rolls, bagels and tortillas
- Dried beans such as kidney beans
- Cereals with low-fat, high-fiber content
- Fruit (especially cantaloupe)
- Pastas
- Grains
- Vegetables and vegetable juices (especially broccoli and green peppers)

To keep your energy up between meals, snack on high-energy snacks and drink plenty of water. Drink as little as possible with your meals to help your digestive system work and get rid of heartburn. Water is an absolutely essential nutrient and our bodies can only survive three or four days without it. But using it to rinse down our food is a very bad habit. Stop drinking with your meals; you'll feel a lot better afterward and eventually not even miss it. Here are some high-energy, healthy snacks: pretzels, popcorn, banana, bagels, peanut butter sandwiches and sunflower seeds.

In addition to water and carbohydrates, bodies require protein and fat as nutrients. However, most people get plenty of these without focusing on them. Focus on what's good for you, and you'll only have so much room for all the rest. In other words, "It's not what you are eating that's killing you, but what you're not." Focus on the positive; it will empower you and energize you!

JUST DO IT

Nike came up with a great advertising slogan with the three simple words, "Just Do It." As long as you say, "I'll start exercising when I feel more energetic," you will not start exercising. You must plant the seed of change first—that's the law of the harvest. To get the energy to exercise, you must begin to exercise. Exercise is the greatest energizer because it not only energizes our body; it energizes our mind as well.

An aerobic exercise that involves bouncing up and down will activate the pituitary gland, flooding the system with endorphins and other neurotransmitters that will energize you. As you feel the effects of these natural chemicals kick in, your mind will think more positively. Your self-talk will change. You'll start saying to yourself, "I feel GREAT."

Reach Out

The better you feel about yourself, the better you'll treat others around you. Just as it's energizing to talk yourself up, telling yourself, "you can do it," it's just as energizing to praise others. Try it. Start complimenting others, and see how much better you feel yourself. You can't encourage somebody else without feeling encouraged yourself. Send a card. Make a call. Give a hug. If you're feeling down, pick someone else up.

The Law of Giving is simple, "Give and *it* shall be given unto you." That simply means, whatever you need, you must first give away. In other words, whatever you want to reap you must plant. I've encouraged a lot of people to go on a volunteer vacation, since I founded Missionary Ventures Canada six years ago, to experience the law of giving first-hand. I've seen these people, who thought they were going to be a blessing to someone else, return from their trip with new energy, new vitality and a whole new outlook on life. Helping to build a school, orphanage or church for someone else had done more for them. To stay energized, energize someone else!

Dead People Can't Smell Roses

No need to travel abroad to help the needy if you don't like to travel. Even if you do, balance your giving by visiting the sick. Visit fewer funeral homes and more hospitals. Give more get-well cards and flowers. "Give me the roses while I live," the old song goes. Hug 12 people every day. Call people just to encourage them.

My oldest brother Dave will be driving down the road and call me from his cell phone. Many times all he says when I answer the phone is, "Ben, I just called to say I love you." Every time he does that, I get tears in my eyes. It means so much to hear those words from someone, especially a brother. I wonder how many other guys in this world get those calls from a brother. I certainly am blessed. Call a sibling right now, and tell them you love them. See how it energizes you!

Pressure and tension draw a blank.

26 Steps to More Energy and Less Stress

1. Learn to relax without feeling guilty.
2. Take a hot bath before bedtime.
3. Take a warm shower every morning.
4. Get a massage once a month.
5. Exercise three to five times a week for 20 to 30 minutes. Work yourself into a sweat. Fitness reduces stress.
6. Don't sweat the small stuff. Keep things in perspective.
7. Take regular vacations.
8. Go to church with your family every week.
9. Help those less fortunate.
10. Drink plenty of water and less caffeine. Don't drink with your meals. Let your saliva do its job.

11. Eat right. More carbohydrates and less fats. Lots of fruits and vegetables.
12. Be grateful. Count your blessings every day.
13. Be enthusiastic!
14. Forgive others to the degree you wish to have forgiveness. Grudges are too heavy to be carried around.
15. Spend time in solitude every day. Meditate and pray.
16. Take time to laugh. Lighten up. Humor heals.
17. When you begin to worry about a situation, think of the worst thing that could happen and say, "so what?"
18. Get to bed earlier if you're not getting enough sleep. Most people sleep a half-hour too long every morning. Arise early.
19. Think positive and be optimistic. Expect the best.
20. Recharge your batteries. Have fun. Get yourself a hobby. Write this as "me time" on your calendar.
21. Set balanced personal goals that make you reach, but not for the stars.
22. Be sure you are following the right road map.
23. Get organized. Develop better time management habits.
24. Learn to say NO with a smile. Don't commit to too many things.
25. Spend lots of quality time with those you love. After you're dead, they won't care how much time you spent at the office.
26. Simplify your life.

Staying energized and eliminating unnecessary stress from our lives is great, but being energized does not necessarily mean we're balanced. In other words we can be bursting with energy and still be headed toward burnout if we allow ourselves to get out of balance.

staying in balance

you've got the controls

It was the first day of training for my private helicopter license. As the hot Arizona sun beat down on the windscreen of our Rotorway Exec 90, beads of sweat trickled down my cheeks. Learning to fly the helicopter was impossible, I thought to myself. My instructor was lean, lanky, 60-year-old Stretch Wolters. Long in the legs, and short on patience. He was going to need some with me.

What makes flying the helicopter such a challenge is that both feet and both hands are working the controls at the same time. Movement of any control means compensation is required with the other three. It's really four, because in the left hand is the collective, which by being raised and lowered changes the pitch of the main rotor blades. But also on the end of the same control is the throttle, which is twisted to add and reduce power. In the right hand is the cyclic, which controls the direction of travel by changing the angle of the swash plate. This is the plate at the top of the main shaft on which the blades rotate. Your feet work the foot pedals, which change the pitch of the tail rotor blades. These prevent you from spinning in circles when you are in a hover.

A hover is a word used to describe the act of using all your skill to go absolutely nowhere. It is remaining motionless at a two feet above the ground. This is where most of your training takes place in a helicopter. First Stretch gave me the foot pedals and let me control the heading of the ship as he taxied up and down the runway. After an hour I thought I was doing pretty well, until he handed me the cyclic. It had looked real easy to me. As I took the cyclic, for a couple of ecstatic seconds I felt I was in control. Then without warning, that little egg beater started to drift from side to side, pitching and rolling, lurching forward and then sliding back, like a hat in the wind.

THe FeeLinG oF BaLance

Every correction I make only amplifies the next error. After a few seconds, which seem like eternity, I hear Stretch's calm voice in my headset: "I've got it." What a relief! Almost before he's finished speaking the ship is back to a motionless hover. Poised for whatever he wants to do next. I can't believe it; he's hardly moving the controls! "What's the secret?" I ask. "It's simple," Stretch says. "It's the sense of balance you're missing. When you know what balance feels like, you'll feel any shift off balance long before you can see it. The sooner you make the correction the smaller it needs to be." "What do you mean?" I asked. "Well, think of yourself standing on a beach ball. In order to stay on top without rolling off, you must continually make small adjustments." It seemed to me he was saying, you can't chase balance, just make the right adjustments and wait. Balance will come to you.

I was getting the picture. We could have all the energy or power we wanted in the engine, but if we went out of balance, we were going to crash. Real quick! I persisted with my training since I wasn't about to give up. Not now. Not after I had spent six months and 340 hours of evenings and Saturdays building myself a helicopter from a 6,000-piece kit. After each lesson, and later as I began flying on my own, I began to see a lot of parallels between flying the helicopter in balance and living life in balance.

Before my burnout I was energized all right, but not balanced. I began to realize that's why I had crashed. I could see how energy without balance is very dangerous. Fuel was important to achieve motion, but balance was critical for level flight. With a few hours of practice, and much yelling by Stretch, I was able to hold that machine in a motionless hover, but not for long. Staying balanced in a hover was one thing, moving forward in a hover-taxi changed everything.

Moving Out

Just when I thought I had everything under control, Stretch said to me, "It's time to take this machine places. But be careful. As soon as we move forward we'll be rolling off the donut of air that's supporting us, so you'll need more power. Because you'll be adding power the ship will want to spin counter-clockwise, so you'll need some right pedal. At the same time, because of the gyroscopic procession of the rotating blades, the machine will want to roll to the right. Make sure you put in some left cyclic, or we'll roll over." Yeah right, I thought to myself. Just when I thought I had this mastered. Just as in life, it's easier to maintain balance if you're not going anywhere. The more you plan to do with your life, the better balanced you'll need to be.

Not only moving forward from a hover, but every time we changed direction, I noticed I needed to adjust the controls. The amazing part was we needed a lot less power facing the wind than when we had a tail wind. We had a lot more lift, which is why aircraft take off into the wind. The same goes for us in everyday life. If we face the winds of turbulence, those challenges we all meet, we'll take flight and soar with the eagles. Stretch made sure I mastered the hover before he let me take the ship to altitude. "If you master the hover in balance, you'll always have something to come back to, when you get into trouble."

Fill 'er Up

The amazing thing I noticed as we climbed to cruising altitude was the fact that we now required only 22 inches of manifold pressure instead of the 26 inches it had taken us to maintain a hover. Flying 90 miles an hour was taking less energy than standing still. This was really neat, I thought, as I began to relax and look around. As I looked down at the instruments to see what they were doing, the helicopter started to plunge into a dive. "Ben, keep your eyes focused on the horizon if you want to fly level," hollered Stretch. "Simply glance at the instrument panel, but stay focused on the horizon." The lesson applies to our lives as well, if we want to fly in balance. We stay focused on our goals by regularly checking the instrument panel.

Those gauges tell us the condition of our families, our relationships, our health, our wealth and our faith. They also tell us how much fuel we have left in our tanks.

The number one cause of aircraft accidents is running out of fuel. Ignore your fuel gauge when you're flying, and you are sure to crash. The same applies to life. Have you been feeling anxious, irritable, tired or depressed lately? Have you been experiencing chest pains, insomnia, indigestion or difficulty breathing? Those may be indicators that it is time to land and refuel. That's right—don't try to fuel in mid-flight. It is absolutely critical that you change activity and location to perform the maintenance your mind, body and spirit will require from time to time. The secret is to know your range of flight, or your limits, and then put some margin between your load and your limit.

THE OPPOSITE OF OVERLOAD

"Margin is the amount allowed beyond that which is needed. It is the opposite of overload. It is something held in reserve for contingencies or unanticipated situations,"[24] says Richard A. Swenson, M.D., who has written a great book entitled *Margin—Restoring Emotional, Physical and Time Reserves to Overloaded Lives.* In it he talks about putting margin into everything from our emotional energy to our physical energy, from our time to our finances. I think of margin as the fuel I leave in my tank when I come in to refuel. Even though I have a flight range of two hours, it is illegal for me to be flying at any time without a reserve of 20 minutes. Start building reserve into your life by simply allowing an extra 10 minutes of travel time to get to appointments, meetings or church. That time won't be wasted if you keep reading material with you at all times, and your level of stress will drop immensely.

Too many people waste their time learning how to manage their stress. It is far wiser to learn how to eliminate the unnecessary stress from your life than to leave it there and try to manage it. There are many useless stressors we put up with every day. Not only put up with, but actually create. The main one is the lack of margin in our

lives. Here are some ideas to put margin into your everyday life:
- Wake up a half-hour earlier to give yourself time alone.
- Wake your children up for school earlier (they'll go to bed earlier).
- Give yourself an extra 10 minutes to commute to work.
- Don't let the gas tank in your car drop below one-quarter.
- Show up early for meetings and appointments.
- Schedule space between meetings.
- Don't leave assignments or reports to the last minute.
- Leave plenty of time to catch your plane (you can always read while you wait).
- Keep some cash reserves.
- Live below your means (spend less than you earn).

Lack of margin is the main cause of distress in our lives.

STRESS

Stress wasn't even talked about until at least the 1950s. That was when Dr. Selye discovered and published the concept. His definition of stress is "the nonspecific response of the body to any demand placed upon it."[25] The most popular thinking defines stress as an unpleasant circumstance or event such as a car accident or financial problems. But stress is our response to the circumstance or event, not the event itself. It is not what's around us, but what is within us.

Not all stress is bad. Our lives would be very boring without any stress at all. Most of us, without realizing it, use stress to our advantage. This is called eustress, and it energizes us incredibly. It is the creativity that comes with a deadline, the joy that comes with the birth of a child and the ecstasy that you experienced on your wedding day. We all need some stress or tension to keep us in tune and balanced. Just as the strings of a guitar need tension to harmonize, we need some tension to live in harmony.

When the stress response becomes negative or destructive it is called distress. This is what most of us mean when we use the word stress. The symptoms of distress are the reason for 50 to 70 percent of visits by patients to general practitioners, says Dr. Hart in his book *Adrenaline and Stress*. Here is a list of commonly accepted symptoms of distress:

- Skin diseases
- Frequent headaches
- Tiredness on waking
- Insomnia
- Memory loss
- Irritability/short temper
- Loss of sense of humor
- Lack of ambition
- The desire to avoid people
- Intestinal disorders (i.e., indigestion, constipation)
- Nervous trembling of hands

The key to smooth flight and living in balance is to get rid of all unnecessary distress and learn to compensate and control the rest, because it's part of life. The faster we wish to move, the better balanced we need to be. When I first fired up my helicopter after spending six months building it, I really didn't know how well the blades were balanced until I revved the engine up to operating rpm. Any imbalance would show up in the form of vibration. These vibrations would be like negative stress, in that, if the vibration wasn't removed, the blades would crack in flight. Not on the ground, but in flight.

PRe-FLiGHt

To prevent taking off with cracked blades, part of the pre-flight inspection is to carefully check for cracks. Are you flying with cracked blades caused by hyperstress in your life? Use your time of solitude every morning to do a pre-flight inspection to look for stress cracks and other hazard conditions that may prevent a safe, smooth, balanced flight. Every pilot uses a checklist before and after each and every flight to ensure safety. These inspections are called pre-flight and post-flight. You may wonder why we need a post-flight if we'll do a pre-fight before the next flight. It's simple. That gives us time for any necessary repairs or maintenance, so that the aircraft is ready when it is needed.

Likewise, each and every one of us needs a checklist at the beginning and end of every day to ensure safe, balanced flight. This is especially true if we plan to make a difference with our lives. If we plan to fly. Planes that will remain grounded don't need pre-flight inspection. People that are going places need a pre-flight before they begin every day. They also need a post-flight at the end of every day. Here is a sample pre-flight checklist you can customize for yourself, and use every day.

PRe-FLIGHt CHeCKLiSt

General Pre-Flight
- Always start pre-flight at least 20 minutes before scheduled departure time. That may mean getting out of bed earlier.
- Always refer to checklist. Don't rely on memory.
- Remove all inspection covers—be honest with yourself. Confess your shortcomings. Acknowledge your strengths. You'll notice both as you inspect.

Inspection point #1. Fitness
- Did you exercise your body yesterday to keep it fit? Do it before moving to the next inspection point.
- Did you drink plenty of water?
- Did you eat healthy foods?
- Have you had a physical checkup lately?
- Did you participate in any habits destructive to your health?
- How is your energy level? Is it time for a vacation?
- Did you feed your mind yesterday, to keep it fit? Read and listen to positive, empowering information every day. (See recommended reading at the back of this book.)
- How much time did you spend in front of the television last

evening?

- Did you use any vocabulary yesterday you wouldn't want your kids to hear?
- How has your attitude been lately? Does it need adjustment?

Inspection point #2. Faith

- Did you pray yesterday?
- Were you thankful? Did you give thanks for all the blessings in your life? For everything that's right? Be grateful for your family, for your spouse, for your children, for your friends, for your health, for your wealth, if you have them. If not, be thankful for your food, your shelter, your mind, your body and nature around you. There's always something to be thankful for!
- Did you ask for help with anything that needs repair in your life? Did you ask your friends for help? Did you ask God for help?
- Have you gone to church with your family in the past few weeks?
- Have you read your Bible lately?
- Did you ask for wisdom yesterday?

Inspection point #3. Family

- How much time did you spend with your children last evening?
- Did you call them if you are not living with them?
- Did you tell one of your children yesterday that you were proud of them?
- Did you tuck them in last night and say a little prayer?
- Did you speak only positive words in their presence?
- Did you touch each one cheek-to-cheek for even a few seconds?
- How are they doing in school?
- When is the last time you sent a *thank-you note* to one of their teachers?
- Have you been on a date with your wife in the past month?
- Have you been on a vacation with her in the past year?
- Have you called your parents in the past week?

Inspection point #4. Friends

- Have you sent someone a card in the past week?
- Did you call a friend yesterday just to encourage them?
- Have you entertained guests in your home in the past month?
- Have started assembling a Mastermind Group or Board of Advisors?
- Did you give 12 hugs yesterday to people outside your family?
- Are you happy with the friends in your inner circle?
- Are there any cracks in your relationships that you can repair by asking for forgiveness?
- Were you a blessing to the people you met yesterday?

Inspection point #5. Finances

- Did you spend 15 minutes yesterday reading something relating to your career/business?
- Did you earn more than you spent yesterday?
- Did you give some away?
- Have you started an investment portfolio?
- Have you set up a registered educational savings plan?
- Did you keep record of all expenses yesterday?
- Did you do anything to reduce your debt load?
- Did you give away some of your time and your knowledge?
- Were you organized and efficient at the office?

WHAT'S YOUR HEADING?

When your inspection is complete, chart your course for the day. Where would you like to go? How will you get there? Refer to your goal list and then plot a line from your destination back to where you are; that will be your course to follow. This will be your heading once you've compensated for crosswinds. Crosswinds blow you off course very easily if you don't compensate for them. Crosswinds may be a marital problem, financial difficulties or any other obstacle you face at the time. You will need to compensate for these to stay on course. You are now ready for takeoff.

Make sure you check that compass. Keep your eyes on the horizon. Today's a brand new day and this flight has never been flown before.

Regularly check your attitude indicator. It is especially important when the horizon is not visible. When your goals are out of sight. When clouds of doubt surround you. It's the only way to stay right side up and avoid a crash.

And, oh yes, remember to stay energized. Keep an eye on your fuel gauge. Always keep a reserve. It makes for safer landings.

Safe flying.

God bless.

NOTES

1 *Fast Company* Magazine, February-March 1999 edition, page 83.

2 Matthew 16:26.

3 Kenneth W. Cooper, M.D., *Aerobics* (New York: M. Evans and Company, 1968), pp. 24-26.

4 Liz E. Pearson, R.D. *When In Doubt, Eat Broccoli* (Penguin Books, 1998).

5 F. Batmanghelidj, M.D. *Your Body's Many Cries for Water* (Global Health Solutions Inc., P.O. Box 3189, Falls Church, VA, 22043, USA).

6 Agatha Thrash, M.D. "The Truth About Caffeine." Pamphlet. Narcotics Foundation Inc., 1976.

7 E. Thelle, NEJM (1983); 308:1454-47; Lacroix, A., NEJM (1986); 315 (16): 977-82.

8 *Practical Cardiology*, 1983: 9 (13).

9 P. Snowden, *American Journal of Public Health*, 1984; 74 (8): 820-3.

10 Dr Hans Diel, H.Sc., MPH and Aileen Ludington, MD. " Ask the Doctor," *Lifeline Magazine*, 1985.

11 *Ibid.*

12 *Ibid.*

13 *Ibid.*

14 *The Financial Post*, January 21, 1995.

15 *The Christian Businessman*, February, 1998.

16 Greg Johnson and Mike Yorkey, *Daddy's Home* (Tyndale House Publishers Inc., 1992), page xvi.

17 The Editors of Rodale Press, *Cut Your Spending in Half Without Settling for Less.* (Rodale Press, Emmaus, PA:, 1994.)

18 Frederic Flach, M.D. *Resilience: Discovering a New Strength at Times of Stress* (New York: Fawcett Columbine, 1988), page 259.

19 Romans 10:17.

20 1 Corinthians 13:13.

21 Hans Selye, M.D., *Stress Without Distress* (New York: New American Library, 1974), page 124.

22 1 Corinthians 13:13.

23 Armand Mayo Nicholi II, "Why Can't I Deal with Depression?" *Christianity Today*, November 11, 1983, page 40.

24 Richard A. Swenson, M.D., *Margin—Restoring Emotional, Physical and Time Reserves to Overloaded Lives*, (NavPress Publishing Group, 1992),

25 Selye, page 14.

Ben's Recommended Reading

- Batmanghelidj, F., M.D. *Your Body's Many Cries for Water.* Global Health Solutions Inc., P.O. Box 3189, Falls Church, VA 22043, USA.
- Brown, Les. *Live Your Dreams.* Avon Books, 1992.
- Callaway, Phil. *Making Life Rich Without Any Money.* Harvest House Publishers, 1998.
- Carlson, Richard. *Don't Sweat The Small Stuff, and It's All Small Stuff.* Hyperion, New York, 1997.
- Carnegie, Dale. *How to Win Friends and Influence People.* New York, Pocket Books, 1994.
- Covey, Stephen R. *The 7 Habits of Highly Effective Families.* Audio.
- Cousins, Norman. *The Anatomy of an Illness.* New York, Bantam, 1986.
- Daniels, Peter J. *How To Reach Your Life Goals.* Honor Books, 1995.
- Davidson, Jeff. *The Complete Idiot's Guide To Goal Setting.* New York, Alpha Books, 1998.
- Fenchuk, Gary W. *Timeless Wisdom.* Cake Eaters Inc., 1995.
- Gray, John. *Men Are from Mars, Women Are from Venus.* Audio.
- Hedges, Burke. *You Inc...Discover The CEO Within.* INTI Publishing, 1996.
- Hill, Napoleon. *Think and Grow Rich.* New York, Fawcett, 1975.
- Johnson, Greg, and Yorkey, Mike. *Daddy's Home.* Tyndale House Publishers, Inc., 1992.
- Kubassek, Ben. *Achieving Life Balance.* (Audio Program). Succeed Communications Inc., 1998.
- Kubassek, Ben. *Succeed Without Burnout.* Eagle Press, 1997.
- MacDonald, Gordon. *Ordering Your Private World.* Nashville, Oliver-Nelson, 1984.
- Mason, John L. *An Enemy Called Average.* Insight International, 1990.
- McNally, David. *The Eagle's Secret.* Delacorte Press, 1998.
- Matyas, Diane. *Performance.* Matyas Lifestyle Services, 1998.
- O'Neil, John R. *The Paradox of Success.* Penguin Putnam Inc., 1993.

- Peterson, Eugene H. *The Message*. NavPress, 1993.
- Rohn, Jim. *7 Strategies for Wealth & Happiness*. Prima Publishing, 1996.
- Saunderson, Roy. *How to Focus on Success*. Recognition Management Institute, 1997.
- Selye, Hans, M.D. *Stress Without Distress*. New York, New American Library, 1974.
- Smalley, Gary, *For Better or for Best*. Harper Paperbacks, 1979.
- Smalley, Gary, and Trent, John. *The Language of Love*. Focus on the Family Publishing, 1988.
- Stanley, Thomas J., and Danko, William D. *The Millionaire Next Door*. Longstreet Press, Inc., 1996.
- Swenson, Dr. Richard A. *Margin—Restoring Emotional, Physical and Time Reserves to Overloaded Lives*. NavPress Publishing Group, 1992.
- Taylor, Harold, *Making Time Work for You*. Stoddart Publishing Co., 1989.
- Tracey, Brian. *Maximum Success*. Audio. New York, Simon & Shuster, 1995.

ABOUT THE AUTHOR

Ben Kubassek is an entrepreneur and the best-selling author of *Succeed Without Burnout* and the audio series *Achieving Life Balance*. He is also a popular keynote speaker, sharing his message of hope and secrets of balanced living in our stressed-out world. His powerful words are capable of moving audiences to tears, laughter and spine-tingling joy.

Ben was born and raised in a religious commune. At the age of 21 he left and started his own business. He became a huge success in business as an electrical/mechanical contractor and builder/land developer but hit burnout at age 28. An experience that would change his life forever.

Ben is married to Elizabeth, and can't get enough of his four children. They live together on a hobby farm just outside Kitchener, Ontario.

For more information on Ben's books, or his speaking services, or to schedule him to speak to your company or organization, you may contact him at:

Succeed Communications Inc.
R.R. #3, Bright, Ontario, Canada, N0J 1B0
Tel: 1-800-801-7264 Fax: (519) 632-8800
www.burnout.net
or e-mail Ben at
kubassek@golden.net

Books that inspire, help and heal

ALSO BY Ben KUBassek —

Succeed Without Burnout
Proven strategies to move your life from Burnout to Balance.

"Overcommitted? Burning the candle at both ends? Overloaded emotionally? Then you need to read Succeed Without Burnout. It offers proven strategies to move you from victim to victor!"

Paul J. Meyer, founder,
Success Motivation Institute Inc.

ISBN 0-9681538-0-1 $15.95 CAN $11.95 US

Achieving Life Balance
How to Succeed Without Burnout.

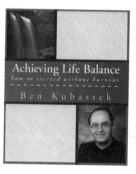

Discover the Powerful Secrets to Living the Five "F"s of Life Balance. The messages on these audio cassettes are filled with profound information on achieving success, with family, friends, fitness, finance and faith.

**Album of 6 audio cassettes   ISBN 0-9681538-1-X
$59.95 CAN $44.95 US**

Call to order:
1-800-287-8610
(toll-free in North America)

or write to:
Creative Bound Inc.
Box 424, Carp, Ontario
Canada K0A 1L0